Xiang Nan: Champion of Reform in Fujian

Li Yang   Zhang Xiaojing

Published by
ACA Publishing Ltd.
University House
11-13 Lower Grosvenor Place
London SW1W 0EX, UK
Tel: +44 (0)20 7834 7676
Fax: +44 (0)20 7973 0076
E-mail: info@alaincharlesasia.com
Web: www.alaincharlesasia.com
Beijing Office
Tel: +86(0)10 8472 1250
Fax: +86(0)10 5885 0639

Authors: Li Yang, Zhang Xiaojing
Editor: David Lammie
Cover art: Daniel Li

Published by ACA Publishing Ltd in association
with the People's Publishing House

© 2016, by People's Publishing House, Beijing, China
ALL RIGHTS RESERVED. NO PART OF THIS
PUBLICATION MAY BE REPRODUCED IN MATERIAL FORM,
BY ANY MEANS, WHETHER GRAPHIC,
ELECTRONIC, MECHANICAL OR OTHER, INCLUDING
PHOTOCOPYING OR INFORMATION STORAGE, IN WHOLE OR IN PART, AND
MAY NOT BE USED TO PREPARE
OTHER PUBLICATIONS WITHOUT WRITTEN
PERMISSION FROM THE PUBLISHER.

The greatest care has been taken to ensure accuracy but the
publisher can accept no responsibility for errors or omissions, or
for any liability occasioned by relying on its content.

ISBN 978-1-910760-10-9

A catalogue record for *Xiang Nan: Champion of Reform in Fujian*
is available from the National Bibliographic Service of the British Library.

Glossary of Terms

CMC	**Central Military Commission**
CPC	**Communist Party of China**
CPG	**central people's government**
CPPCC	**Chinese people's political consultative conference**
KMT	**Kuomintang (Nationalist Party)**
NGO	**non-government organisation**
NPC	**national people's congress**
PLA	**People's Liberation Army**
PRC	**People's Republic of China**
SEZ	**special economic zone**
SOE	**state-owned enterprise**
SDPC	**state development planning commission**
SPC	**state planning commission**
TCM	**traditional Chinese medicine**

Democratic figures/personages refer to people of note who are 'members of non-CPC political parties'

Preface

The reform and opening up of China ushered in the socialist road with Chinese characteristics and sparked the dawn of a new era. The immortal and meritorious services of Deng Xiaoping, the initiator, chief designer and commander-in-chief of that road, will be eternally engraved on the minds of the Chinese people. He accomplished these outstanding feats with his selfless comrades-in-arms and senior army generals blazing a trail, and going through fire and water with him. The founding fathers and commanders-in-chief of the reform and opening up prompted hundreds of millions of Chinese people to embark together on the new journey that we are still following today. Their eminent contributions deserve to be documented and their deeds should be remembered and admired. They are the role models and examples for the broad masses of party members and cadres to follow on the new journey of reform and opening up.

To cherish the memory of these founding fathers of reform and opening up and to enable readers, especially party members and cadres, to know them better and to learn from them as role models, we decided to publish the *Pictorial Biographies of the Founding Fathers of China's Reform and Opening Up* series. To present these books to readers at the earliest opportunity, we will publish this series volume by volume as each book is completed.

China has entered a new era of reform and opening up. The party central committee with comrade Xi Jinping as general secretary has declared the epoch-making new manifesto of reform and opening up. The implementation of the manifesto requires the devotion and joint efforts of brave generals keeping pace with the times, losing no time moving ahead, fearing no upheavals, abolishing outdated laws and regulations, and defying the negative statements of others; it requires innumerable cadres hurling themselves into the reform and opening-up process; and it requires the collective efforts of hundreds of millions of people. Only in this way can our great cause keep on advancing!

People's Publishing House, August 2014

Alain Charles Asia (ACA) Publishing Ltd is delighted to be associated with the People's Publishing House to bring this book to an English-speaking readership.

ACA, formerly known as ACP (Alain Charles Publishing) Ltd Beijing, was founded in October 1989 and was the first foreign-owned publishing company to be allowed to open an office in China.

In 2007, ACP Beijing was renamed ACA Publishing Ltd to better reflect its focus on China and the Asia-Pacific region. The company specialises in publishing books about China for international readers and has offices in Beijing and London.

ACA Publishing Ltd, October 2016

Contents

Chapter 1   A 12-year-old Young Pioneer Squad Leader Arrives in Shanghai and Nanjing..................1

Chapter 2   Red Tales of the Xiang Family..................9

Chapter 3   Setting up the 'Tomorrow' Singing Troupe in Changle County...18

Chapter 4   Attempting Repeatedly to Create Anti-Japanese Propaganda Groups..................21

Chapter 5   Rejoining the Party After a Transfer to Northern Jiangsu.......26

Chapter 6   Love in Time of War..................30

Chapter 7   'If That Bridge is Not Up and Running by Nightfall, I Will Have You Shot'..................36

Chapter 8   Entering the Youth League Apparatus..................40

Chapter 9   Xiang Nan Finds Xiang Nan..................51

Chapter 10   Reunited with his Long-lost Mother..................53

Chapter 11   A First Foreign Visit to the USSR..................61

Chapter 12   A Capable Assistant to Hu Yaobang, Top Leader of the Youth League..................66

Chapter 13   Reuniting with his Father in Shenyang..................70

Chapter 14   Luckily Escaping the Misfortune of Being Branded a Rightist....77

Chapter 15   Attending the Sixth World Youth Friendship Festival..........83

Chapter 16   Suddenly Face to Face With the 'Anti-Right Deviation' Storm....87

Chapter 17   Sent Down to Labour in the Beijing Dongjiao State Farm........97

Chapter 18   The Courage and Insight of Minister Chen Zhengren..........107

Chapter 19 Compiling a Series of Research Reports on Agricultural Mechanisation..111

Chapter 20 A Year on the Ground at the Luoyang Tractor Factory............116

Chapter 21 The 'Xinzhou Experience' and the Ideals of Agricultural Mechanisation..118

Chapter 22 The Nightmare Years of the 'Cultural Revolution'..................123

Chapter 23 A Path-breaker in the Liberation of Thinking......................130

Chapter 24 Assigned as Ambassador to the Frontier with Deng Xiaoping's Support..146

Chapter 25 The Most Urgent Task in Fujian is the Liberation of Thinking...151

Chapter 26 Taking up the Responsibility System for Agrarian Production, as a Breakthrough Tool..154

Chapter 27 'Making an SEZ is Imperative'.......................................162

Chapter 28 The Nation's First 10,000-Line Digital-Switching Telephone System..166

Chapter 29 Using Foreign Investment as Wings for the SEZ's Smooth Takeoff..168

Chapter 30 Establishing the First Sino-Foreign Joint Venture Company....176

Chapter 31 Thoroughly Redressing the Wrongful Cases Against Fujian's Underground Party Workers...183

Chapter 32 Implementing Policies for the Renowned Son of China and Entrepreneur Aw Boon Haw..189

Chapter 33 Resolutely Combating Smuggling and Trafficking in Smuggled Goods...193

Chapter 34 'Fujian's Economy Relies on TVEs as the Spearhead'............196

Chapter 35 'The Classic of Mountains and Sea' at the Frontier Extends Its Influence Across the Nation..201

Chapter 36 Deng Xiaoping Inspects Xiamen SEZ, and Xiang Nan Bravely Speaks Up..205

Chapter 37 Breaking Through Layers of Obstruction to Recruit Foreign-Invested Projects..215

Chapter 38 Deciding the Fate of Enterprises by Loosening Administrative Approval Processes...219

Chapter 39 The Controversy over 'Jinjiang Fake Medicines'.....................227

Chapter 40 With Deep Feeling, Bidding Farewell to Fujian at 67..............233

Chapter 41 Founding and Leading the China Foundation for the Alleviation of Poverty..245

Chapter 42 A Monument to the Alleviation of Poverty Stands in People's Hearts..257

Epilogue..274

Chronology of Major Events in the Life of Xiang Nan............................276

Chapter 1

A 12-year-old Young Pioneer Squad Leader Arrives in Shanghai and Nanjing

Xiang Nan was born in the village of Wendi in the township of Pengkou, Liancheng county, Fujian province, on 18 November 1918. In keeping with family tradition, he was called Xiang Dechong (项德崇). Later, when he joined the New Fourth Army, he changed his name to Xiang Nan.

The village of Wendi is situated in a mountainous region. Only by crossing a number of large hills and walking for several tens of miles on mountain paths could the larger village of Wenfang be reached.

Xiang Nan's ancestral home in Wendi village, Pengkou township, Liancheng county, Fujian province

Xiang Nan's home village of Wenfang in Pengkou township, Liancheng county, Fujian province

According to tradition, in the reign of the Jiaxi emperor of the Song dynasty (1237-1240), a commander, Xiang Anren, in Taixing county in the province of Zhejiang, followed Wen Tianxiang[1] in raising an army to resist the Mongol invading forces. Under attack by the Mongol army, they retreated towards Liancheng, but, as they moved through the village of Wenfang, Xiang Anren left an infant grandson, Siliu, still in swaddling clothes, in the care of an old couple whose family name was Wen. Xiang Anren followed Wen Tianxiang into Guangdong province, and their final fate was unknown, but the infant left behind with the old couple grew to adulthood and became the first descendant of the Xiang clan in Liancheng. To commemorate what Wen Tianxiang and this elderly couple had done in caring for this infant, the members of the Xiang clan later renamed their village Wenfang.

The members of the Xiang family acquired fields in the nearby village of Wendi. Wenfang was a large village, and the Xiang clan's private academy for the instruction of young family members was located there. At the age of five, Xiang Nan entered the family academy, where his teacher was Xiang Jishen.

As a youth, Xiang Nan often moved back and forth among the mountain villages. Even as a small child he would be in charge of the water buffalo or would gather firewood; sometimes, searching for a lost water buffalo, he could be seen late at night walking along the mountain paths by lantern light.

The compound in Wendi village, where Xiang Nan was born

The Xiang clan temple in Wenfang village

One day in 1927, in the village of Wenfang, Xiang Nan saw a column of armed men coming out of the village along the road. At the Xiang family temple, he watched the leader of these armed men marching in close quarters with the troops. Later on he came to realise that they were preparing to raise an uprising in the Guangdong region of Chaoshan, following the 'Nanchang uprising', and that the leader of the troops was the man who would later become the commander of the Fourth Red Army, Zhu De.

As a child he left home; as an elder he returned: Xiang Nan in Wenfang, 1986

The western part of Fujian province was red territory. After 1927, Deng Zihui, Zhang Dingcheng, Guo Diren and others planted the seeds of revolution in western Fujian, setting off a series of violent peasant incidents. Later, when the Fourth Red Army took places such as Changting, Longyan and Yongding, the revolutionary situation in Fujian seemed to reach a high tide. In the area that embraced Changting, Shanghang and Liancheng, a soviet government was set up; Wenfang became one of the earliest places in China to establish this soviet form of government.

A 12-year-old Young Pioneer SquadLeader Arrives in Shanghai and Nanjing

Xiang Nan and his wife, Wang Zhisheng, enjoy a friendly chat with family members in Wenfang

The only photograph of Xiang Nan with his mother and younger sister, taken in Shanghai in the early 1930s

Xiang Nan's sixth uncle and his father had travelled to Beijing (which was known as Beiping before the communist government came to power in 1949) and Shanghai to work, along with the third elder brother, Xiang Tingjue. But now they returned to their home to join the Red Army. Under the influence of the sixth uncle, and after the establishment of the soviet in Wenfang, Xiang Nan became the leader of a Young Pioneer squad, routinely carrying a spear and manning a roadside checkpoint at the entrance to the village. The sixth uncle was killed in an attack on Liancheng, his body cut into four pieces and hung from the four gates of the city. The sacrifice of the sixth uncle left Xiang Nan with an early understanding of the bitter tragedy that came with revolutionary struggle.

Xiang Nan and his wife Wang Zhixin chat informally with friends in the Xiang family's native village

One day late in 1929, when Xiang Nan was 11 years old, his mother excitedly told him that his father had sent a message and some money to them in the care of a fellow countryman, asking them to come to Shanghai. For Xiang Nan, this news exceeded his fondest dreams.

A 12-year-old Young Pioneer SquadLeader Arrives in Shanghai and Nanjing

The site of Yaohuamen primary school in Nanjing, now called the Nanjing City Qixia District central primary school (photo by Xia Meng)

In the autumn of 1930, Xiang Nan and his mother Wang Cunyu, a Hakka peasant who had never before left home, along with his little sister, left their old family home, and after arduous travel, finally arrived in Shanghai to reunite with Xiang Nan's father.

Xiang Nan finally could see his father, Xiang Yunian, from whom he had been separated for so long. His father, tall and with a severe demeanour, seemed unfamiliar to the boy. But father and son had very few opportunities to spend time together, and Xiang Nan did not even know what his father did for a living – he could only watch him coming and going. His father always seemed in a hurry, leaving at the break of day and returning late at night.

They had not been living long in their typical Shanghai Shikumen house when Xiang Nan was sent by his father to attend Yaohuamen primary school in Nanjing. This school had been established under the watchful eye of Tao Xingzhi, and some of his sayings were hung on its walls, such as "Life is education, society is our school", "The two treasures of life are the two hands and the brain", and "We must take a stand against book learning detached from reality, against pedantry and against hopeless enslavement to our books". The renowned Tao Xingzhi carried a large fan made from a palm leaf when he lectured to his students, leaving a very deep impression on the young Xiang Nan.

Most of the students in this school were the sons of poor families. Xiang Nan had had two years of schooling in the family private academy, and went directly into the fifth-year class of his new primary school, but most of the students in his class were much older and while Xiang Nan could speak in the Hakka language, he could not utter a word in the national dialect spoken by his fellow students.

After school, he often hung around in the busy schoolyard with other students and adults. The quiet library at school became Xiang Nan's paradise. Not only could he find books to read there, but he also could read newspapers each day from the first page to the last. At those times, when he was alone and not surrounded by others, he could read aloud, trying to make his accent sound like that of his classmates with its particular Nanjing flavour.

After two years, he returned to Shanghai and entered into an art school known as the Shanghai Qiangshu. At about this time, his father suddenly left Shanghai.

Chapter 2

Red Tales of the Xiang Family

Xiang Nan recalled many powerful memories from his youth in Shanghai. In particular, in the courtyard of their traditional Shanghai-style Shikumen home on the Rue Vouillemont in the city's French Concession, his father and others came and went, seemingly very busy. At the time, he thought it somewhat strange – what could all these older men be up to? His father had said nothing to him about this, and the young Xiang Nan dared not ask. Xiang Nan loved going to the cinema, and a favourite uncle with a big beard often took him. Later, though, in the middle of a single night, his bearded uncle and the other uncles disappeared without trace.

A photo presented to Mo Xiong by Xiang Yunian in 1956. Underneath the photo, Mo Xiong wrote the following words: 'Comrade Liang Mingde, who guided the path to revolution'

One day in 1934, his father, with a strange and distracted look on his face, bade farewell to Xiang Nan's mother. From then on, he sent neither word nor letter.

On another day, as Xiang Nan returned home from the Qiangshu arts school, a neighbour told him tensely that he had better leave at once, for his mother and little sister had been taken away by the police.

At that time, Xiang Nan had no idea that his home was a top liaison venue for the central leadership of the Communist Party. Only many years later did he learn that his mother, living there, was the keeper of a secret broadcasting station of the Communist Party of China (CPC) leadership.

Xiang Nan's father, Xiang Yunian, was originally called Xiang Tingchun, and later changed his name to Liang Mingde. When he was 15, he was married to his child bride Wang Cunyu in their home village. But soon after the marriage, he and his third brother Xiang Tingjue left for the excitement of Beijing and Shanghai.

This third brother Xiang Tinjue was a graduate of the Fujian School of Law and Government, and had held a post with the army of the northern warlords known as the Beiyang Army. When he heard that Sun Yat-sen was building a national revolution in Guangdong province, and was preparing a military expedition to move northwards against the northern generals, he took Xiang Yunian with him and headed south to throw themselves into the revolution. Received and helped by Sun Yat-sen's personal arrangements, Xiang Yunian and the third brother became deputy-level platoon leaders under Xu Chongzhi, commander of the Second Revolutionary Army. Then, in one of the national revolution's lowest moments, Chen Jiongming rebelled, and the northern expedition failed and receded. Chaotic war ensued between the old warlords of the north and the new militarists in the south. Xiang Yunian realised that the KMT was riddled with factions and struggling among themselves for power and profit. His heart sank in disappointment.

In the spring of 1925, Xiang Yunian and a close friend who called himself Xuan Zheng left Guangzhou and lodged with Xuan Zheng's father at his silk business in Hangzhou. Xuan Zheng's father was a man of progressive ideas, sympathetic to the revolution. His business premises were also one of the CPC central leaders' liaison locations. Here, Xiang Yunian met the party members, Xuan Zhonghua and He Chihua, and, under their influence, Xiang imbibed the ideas of communism. That autumn, in a room at Zhejiang Xiashi primary school, Xiang secretly took the oath and became a member of the CPC.

In January 1926, the KMT held its second national congress in Guangzhou. Because Xiang Yunian was very familiar with the situation in Guangdong province, Xuan Zhonghua brought him along to the congress, and he sent a message to Zhou Enlai and Deng Yingchao, introducing Xiang. Quick-witted and diligent, Xiang Yunian won a positive appraisal from Zhou.

After the April 12 incident,[1] Xiang Yunian lost contact with the party. Luckily, his identity was not revealed; after a short while, he was able to find the party organisation again, and thus became a member of party central's special department.[2]

In 1956, Premier Zhou Enlai instructed Li Kenong to send Xiang Yunian on a special mission to Guangdong to invite Mo Xiong to join the national day celebrations there. Here, Xiang Yunian and Mo Xiong stand in front of Mo's residence

In 1933, Xiang Yunian was working in Shanghai for the party's central military commission, carrying out intelligence work and liaison among top party leaders under the leadership of Wang Shiying and Liu Zihua.

In that year and in 1934, the main tasks of the central military commission were to coordinate the efforts of the Red Army aimed at disrupting the KMT's 'encirclement campaigns' against the communists' soviet areas. Many comrades, including Xiang Yunian, were sent to the soviet in Jiangxi province, and established underground organisations and conducted united front operations in Nanchang, Jiujiang and De'an. They also planned military attacks on the KMT, bombing railways, bridges and airfields.

In 1960, while in Sanya, Hainan on a health sojourn, Zhou Enlai met with Xiang Yunian and presented him with this precious photo. The picture shows Zhou Enlai and Deng Yingchao receiving Xiang Yunian (ninth from right in the second row) with other comrades

On 25 September 1993, Chiang Kai-shek assembled a force of a million men and began his 'fifth annihilation campaign' against several soviet base areas. He threw half a million soldiers into the campaign aimed at the central soviet in Jiangxi. Having seen his first four campaigns end in failure, Chiang adopted a new strategy for the fifth effort: instead of driving straight into the heart of the soviet, as he had tried to do before, this time he decided on a step-by-step encircling approach, building an ever-narrowing string of blockhouses and guard towers as his forces advanced, hoping to strangle the soviet area and dissolve the survivability of the Red Army. He aimed at a final decisive battle against the Red Army's main force so as to gain his ultimate objective – the destruction of the Red Army.

After a year of bitter warfare, the Red Army was unable to break the enemy's encirclement. In order to hasten the demolition of the main Red Army and occupy the central party leadership's soviet area, Chiang called a top-secret conference at Lushan in early October 1934 to plan for the decisive military engagement, and plot the details of the so-called 'iron drum' strategy. The special representative of the fourth district of northern Jiangxi, in De'an county, and the security commander of that district, whose name was Mo Xiong, attended this secret military conference in Lushan.

The conference went on for a week. Chiang Kai-shek personally took a detailed leadership role in planning the military moves. He intended to use 1.5m troops in a sudden encirclement drive, surrounding the CPC leaders' base, which was headquartered in Ruijin. The cordon would first be drawn at a radius of 150km from Ruijin.

Xiang Yunian (middle row, third from right) with Zhou Enlai and Deng Yingchao at Sanya

Chiang's war plans were very precise; the documents coming out of the Lushan planning conference weighed as much as 6.8kg. Each document bore the stamp 'Top Secret', and each was assigned a specific number to accord with its title. On the maps, a complex matrix showed which force, and which small unit, should be in exactly which place at exactly what time, and what barbed wire nets, what incendiary networks and what fortifications were to be used. Once the encirclement was complete, the advance towards Ruijin would begin, with good discipline and under the strictest command.

When the planning conference was over, Mo Xiong returned to his security command headquarters in De'an. Before he had even washed or changed his clothes, he called the three secret members of the Communist Party, Liu Yafo, Lu Zhiying and Xiang Yunan, into his office. He ordered his guards to leave, shut the door, and passed to them the documents from the Lushan military planning conference. The three men scanned the materials for an hour or so and hurriedly concluded. They exchanged glances, and Liu Yafo said to Mo Xiong: "Elder Brother, what do we do next?"

Mo replied: "Isn't there still a way to deal with this? With a crisis this urgent, you have to figure out a way to inform the Red Army!" The three men stood up as one and said in resolute tones: "On behalf of the party, we thank you!"

In 1978, the party committee of Longyan city conducted a commemorative service in honour of Xiang Yunian

Then they decided to send the documents with Xiang Yunian to the security command headquarters rear area administration offices in Nanchang. There, Xiang was to contact several top underground party workers, who could copy the main contents of the Lushan documents and send them by telegraph to the Communist Party leaders, conveying the main elements of the KMT's impending 'iron barrel encirclement' campaign. All that night, they worked with specially concocted fluids to copy the secret codes used in the KMT's war plans, writing the codes secretly into four student dictionaries.

Xiang Yunian was closely familiar with the geography of the soviet. He assumed the identity of a teacher, carrying the dictionaries, and by night made his way toward the central soviet area. To avoid encounters with the enemy at roadblocks, he concealed himself by day and moved only at night. He went without food and moved through the mountains in order to avoid the main roads. After several days, his body was stretched to the limit, and he had walked to the point of exhaustion. The closer he came to the soviet region, the tighter the enemy's blockade became. On his final effort to move through the blockade, Xiang Yunian struck out into the forest, and with a chunk of stone smashed out four of his front teeth. He nearly collapsed from the pain and loss of blood. But by doing this, he managed to complete his transformation into a beggar, and was able to stagger along through layer after layer of the enemy's blockade lines. Finally, on the sixth day, he reached Ruijin, and was able to place in Zhou Enlai's own hands this vital information so significant to the entire course of the revolution.

In 1978, the CPC's Liaoning provincial committee held a memorial service for Xiang Yunian

Xiang Nan and his wife clean the casket of his father in Longyan, 1994

Several days later, with the KMT encirclement of the soviet area still not completely sealed, the party's leaders led their Red Army forces on their initial departure from the central soviet, setting out on the road to the Long March.

In 1949, just after the liberation of Guangzhou, the secretary of the Guangdong provincial party committee, Ye Jianying, sent a representative to find Mo Xiong in Hong Kong and convey Mao Zedong's best wishes to him. Ye Jianying said of Mo: "Before we moved toward the south, Chairman Mao said to me: 'Do you still remember someone named Mo Xiong in Guangdong?'

"I answered: 'I do indeed.'

"Chairman Mao said: 'He is an old friend of our party, and an old comrade. You must go looking for him. It doesn't matter what he might have done wrong, we must set up a good job for him in the party'."

Nor did Zhou Enlai ever forget the contributions of Mo Xiong, Xiang Yunian and others to the revolution. In 1956, Xiang Yunian was designated by Zhou Enlai and by General Li Kenong, head of the party centre's

Xiang Nan bears the casket containing the ashes of his father at Xiang Yunian's memorial service. On the right is Mme Wu Jian, who married Xiang Yunian when they were in Yan'an

committee's investigations department and deputy chief of the PLA general staff, to travel to Guangzhou and accompany Mo Xiong to Beijing for China's national day celebrations.

Chapter 3

Setting up the 'Tomorrow' Singing Troupe in Changle County

Finding himself homeless, with his mother and younger sister taken away to Shanghai's Tilanqiao prison, the best Xiang Nan could do for himself was to find a low-level job copying and writing for a magazine published by the China vocational education association. At the same time, he continued to study at the Qiangshu arts school, which was run by the same association. He spent two years in this part-work, part-study situation.

In 1937, bearing a letter of introduction from the vocational education association, the 19-year-old Xiang Nan left Shanghai for Changle county in Fujian province. There, for the first time in his life, he found a regular job, working in a plant nursery run by the Changle county government.

At that time, the Changle county magistrate Wang Boqiu also held the post of special commissioner in the Fujian provincial government first administrative office. Wang was a supporter of 'government by good men', an idea he shared with prominent intellectuals such as Hu Shi and Li Dazhao. In Changle, Wang Boqiu worked to improve county administration, building roads, planting trees and sprucing up the appearance of the county capital. He promoted education for

Xiang Nan in 1937, employed at a plant nursery in Changle

the humble people, established a 'hall of education for the masses' and paid special attention to opening the minds of the people through education. In these ways, the entire climate of Changle was refreshed.

Soon after, the July 7 Incident occurred in Beijing.[1] The entire country was swept up in a furious determination to resist the Japanese and save the nation from extinction. In Changle, Xiang Nan quickly joined his fellow natives of Liancheng county who were serving in the Changle government, Luo Shusheng and Luo Xinru, and with Chen Yiyun, the head of the local hall of education, to throw themselves into various activities in support of the cause of resisting Japan and saving the nation. They reasoned that the best way to awaken the masses to the cause would be through the use of singing and theatrical performances. And so they quickly set up a 'Singing Troupe for Tomorrow'. Xiang Nan himself wrote the troupe's signature song, the first lines of which are 'Tomorrow! Tomorrow! Tomorrow, tomorrow, victorious tomorrow! We must rescue the nation, we must fight the resistance war…'

Xiang Nan (right) with two of his friends from the 'Resist Japan and Save the Nation' movement, in Fuzhou, 1937

The singing troupe's activities won the support of Wang Boqiu. Wang had a high opinion of Xiang Nan, who had demonstrated a lively intelligence and strong organisational abilities. Under the name of the 'Changle County

Rear Area Association to Support the War of Resistance', Wang provided funds to the singing troupe. Xiang Nan tried to solicit funds everywhere he went, and even contributed some of his own savings to help cover the troupe's costs.

The singing troupe soon aroused a strong response among young people with some formal education. Not only did some progressively minded youth in Changle step forward; the troupe even found support among educated young people and uprooted university students in the provincial capital of Fuzhou who had fled from their homes in Beijing and Tianjin.

The Singing Troupe for Tomorrow put on skits and sang songs about national salvation and resisting Japan, but they also spent time improving their reading skills and discussing current events. They performed often, in rural villages outside the county capital and in schools. Their propaganda work for the cause of anti-Japanese resistance and national salvation was lively and colourful, but it soon caught the attention of the KMT's secret police. After Wang Boqiu was transferred elsewhere, the Singing Troupe for Tomorrow had no way to survive, and was compelled to announce its disbandment.

Chapter 4

Attempting Repeatedly to Create Anti-Japanese Propaganda Groups

The conspicuous achievements of Xiang Nan's propaganda work in Changle county came to the attention of Wang Zhu, who headed the Communist Party's propaganda section in Fujian province. At this time, the office of the New Fourth Army had publicly opened in Huangxiang in the city of Fuzhou. Wang Zhu headed the office. He sent an emissary to Xiang Nan, encouraging Xiang to continue his work of rallying progressive young people to the cause and pursuing his work in support of anti-Japanese resistance. In 1938, Wang Zhu introduced Xiang Nan to membership in the CPC.

Xiang Nan's guide on the revolutionary path, Wang Zhu, was a native of Tingjiang in Fuzhou. Early in his career, he studied at Yanjing University in Beijing. He became a Communist Party member in 1931. He held successive posts as deputy head of the political section of the New Fourth Army's district in Fujian, Zhejiang and Jiangxi, political commissar of the independent brigade in northern Fujian, head of the propaganda section and concurrently head of the united front section in the party's special commission for eastern Fujian, and chief of the New Fourth Army's office in Fuzhou. On 21 September 1941, bandits attacked him and the troops with whom he was travelling at Dongkengtou in Jianyang, and Wang was unfortunately killed

Xiang Nan (second row, third from left) with the travelling team for popular education in Minqing county, 1938

Early that summer, the war situation turned extremely tense in Fujian. The provincial government evacuated inland to Yongan, and vast numbers of civilians from the towns and villages along the coast also fled towards the interior. Xiang Nan's countryman Luo Shusheng was transferred to be the magistrate of Shunchang county, and Xiang Nan and Luo Xinru joined him there. Xiang Nan continued his employment as a gardener under the county government while building up 'resistance and salvation' activities at the instruction of Wang Zhu. After Shanghai fell to the Japanese, he organised some of the uprooted Shanghai young people in a 'Shunchang Fight the Enemy Theatre Troupe', which staged performances for audiences of common people.

It was not long before the KMT secret police turned their eyes toward Xiang Nan's activities in Shunchang. One day, just as Luo Xinru was going to work at the county government, the head of the KMT's seventh security detachment, Xu Guojun, called on Magistrate Luo Shusheng. Xu said: "We already know that Xiang Dechong and others are members of the Communist Party." After Xu departed, Luo Shusheng told Luo Xinru to get an urgent message to Xiang Nan, ordering him to go on the run. A few hours later, Xu Guojun led a group of his security forces to Xiang Nan's home to take Xiang into custody, but they found it empty.

After Xiang Nan fled from Shunchang, he hid out for a time in Fuzhou. In the late spring and early summer of 1939, at the invitation of Huang Kaixiu, an inspector in the Minqing county education bureau, Xiang Nan proceeded to Minqing, and joined with others in forming a so-called 'working team for popular education activities in time of war'. Xiang Nan himself was the team leader, and Huang Kaixiu served as an advisor. Thanks to the efforts of Huang Kaixiu, the Minqing county government decided to provide funds, and agreed that Xiang Nan's 'working team' could continue its activities under the county government's name. After the perils he had undergone in Shunchang, Xiang Nan now changed his name to Xiang Xin, and carried on his duties with greater caution than before.

The Minqing county government mobile 'working team for popular education in time of war' established a school for the people, and organised a 'reading association' and a performance troupe. They went into the mountain villages to carry the message of anti-Japanese resistance in a colourful and lively manner.

Three friends amid the flames of war. Xiang Nan and comrades in Minqing, Fujian

In the spring of 1939, the CPC Fujian provincial committee sent Xiang Nan to Minqing county to lead the campaign of resistance to Japan and national salvation. Placed on the authorities' 'most wanted' list, Xiang Nan hid at Honglincuo (pictured here) and continued his secret operations, including the establishment of the publications *Resist Japan and Save the Nation Weekly* and *Minqing Bulletin*. Finally, thanks to the support of the population, he was able to escape

It is not clear whether it was the mobile working team's activities or Xiang Nan personally who excited the concerns of the authorities. The head of the Minqing county police, Li Jianbang, sent out the order to have Xiang Nan arrested, establishing roadblocks and checkpoints on all roads and at all piers. Huang Kaixiu was able to get a warning to Xiang Nan, and managed to conceal him for a time at a building called Hunglincuo, which belonged to Huang's family. After two or three months, the gale subsided, and Huang Kaixiu personally dispatched Xiang Nan on a tiny river steamer northwards to Nanping.

Xiang Nan stayed for a few months in Nanping, but with no word of Wang Zhu's whereabouts, he had no choice but to leave Fujian and move towards Guilin, in the hope that the Eighth Route Army office there would arrange his transfer on to Yan'an.

Attempting Repeatedly to Create Anti-Japanese Propaganda Groups

Xiang Nan with members of the 'Minqing working team for popular education during the war of resistance against Japan', reunited in Meicheng in December 1984

Chapter 5

Rejoining the Party After a Transfer to Northern Jiangsu

Xiang Nan reached Guilin in the autumn of 1939, and made contact with the Eighth Route Army office there. Because the KMT had tightened its blockade and other controls, there was no way for him to move on to Yan'an.

The Guilin office of the Eighth Route Army, 1939 (photo by Tong Xiaopeng)

Xiang Nan's life was unsteady. A comrade in the Eighth Route Army told him: "The Chengda normal school in Guilin is looking for a biology teacher – why don't you give it a try?"

Xiang Nan replied: "I never studied biology; how could I teach it?"

The comrade answered: "Don't worry. I'll teach you a class and then you can teach it to the students." And that is how it came to pass that Xiang Nan was hired as a biology teacher at Chengda normal school. He would chuckle about it later: a biology instructor who had never studied the subject.

One day, walking in a corridor, humming a song from the film *Children of Troubled Times*, some students overheard him and begged him to teach them singing. That was much easier than teaching biology, so in his classroom he taught his students to sing the main songs from that famous film. That quickly came to the attention of the school authorities, who were nearly certain that Xiang Nan belonged to the CPC. With that, Xiang Nan was sacked.

At about that time, Xiang Nan's thoughts returned to the Chinese vocational education society. He sought out a well-known society member from his own home town, Zhang Xuecheng, and Zhang provided him with an introduction to the director of the Guilin botanical nursery. With his modest monthly income there, he could not only support himself but even provide a little financial help to seven or eight uprooted youngsters in Guilin. Late in his life, Xiang Nan would say with a laugh that, at prevailing prices in those days, that was the highest income he received in his entire life.

After six months in Guilin, the Eighth Route Army office decided to move Xiang Nan and a group of comrades aiming to go to Yan'an to Hong Kong, and from there to northern Jiangsu province to join the New Fourth Army.

The man in charge of Eighth Route Army work in Hong Kong was Liao Chengzhi. Everyone was fond of this jolly 'chubby one'. The Hong Kong office's finances were stretched thin; each person received only a little humble food. Seeing this, Liao Chengzhi said: "Aren't you dejected, sitting around the office all day like this? Go ahead out to a coffee house."

Everyone thought: "We don't have any money for food; how are we supposed to have money for a coffee house?"

Xiang Nan in Guilin, 1980. He never forgot the old days in Guilin

Liao Chengzhi laughed. "Let me tell you a secret," he said. "In Hong Kong's coffee houses, they only charge for the coffee. The sugar is free. You can go and sit there gossiping for half the day and gobble free sugar: what are you waiting for?"

And so, every day, Xiang Nan and all the others would lounge in the coffee houses. When they were hungry, they dropped some sugar into a cup of water. Soon they would return home, their bellies full of sugary water. At night, their stomachs would grumble and groan. Years later, Xiang Nan's stomach would rebel at the mere sight of white sugar.

As spring merged with summer in 1941, Xiang Nan and the others dispatched by Liao Chengzhi moved by steamer from Hong Kong to Shanghai. From Shanghai, they travelled on a small cargo boat provided by comrades in the party underground, and made their way to northern Jiangsu.

Fresh from the South Anhui incident,[1] the New Fourth Army by March 1941 had rebuilt a new military headquarters at Yancheng, in northern Jiangsu, a region known in Chinese as Subei. The new headquarters took a very severe view of newly arriving volunteers. Because they could not make contact with Wang Zhu, who had brought Xiang Nan into the party, and given that Xiang Nan had been out of contact with the party organisation, he had no way to prove that he was already a party member. Nevertheless, Zeng Shan, who headed the organisation department of the party's central China bureau, received Xiang Nan warmly, and assigned him to work in the party committee at Yanfu.

His inability to verify his party membership meant that Xiang Nan could not participate in organisational work of any kind. Cao Diqiu, who headed the popular mobilisation department in Yanfu, recommended that Xiang Nan join the party all over again while he was waiting for proof of his original connection to the party organisation, to save time. Xiang Nan accepted the idea and went through the party membership procedures again in 1941, this time becoming a party member in Subei.

After that, Xiang Nan was dispatched to Fudong, in Yanfu district. The county of Fudong was created after Huang Kecheng's forces took over the Subei area, under the Yanfu administrative authorities. The county administered several lower-level districts, including Dongkan and Sanba.

Chapter 6

Love in Time of War

In 1942, as part of the effort to fight back against the Japanese army's 'cleansing operation' in Subei, Wang Zhixin, a young girl student at the 'Anti-Japan No. 5 school', was sent to work in the region controlled by the New Fourth Army. It was already dark by the time Wang and her fellow female students reached Fudong to report for duty.

Xiang Nan (far left) when serving as secretary of Fudong county government in 1942

Early the next morning, Wang Zhixin was awakened by the sound of someone whistling in the courtyard. She had been accustomed to that form of reveille at her school. Opening the door, she gazed upon a young cadre, clad in a black cotton gown, whistling the call to muster. She was drawn to this handsome cadre, whose appearance was so very different from other soldiers. His attire was half-native, and certainly not western. Around his waist, he wore not the usual military belt but a hemp rope. She was not sure why, but somehow this young man's carelessness about his appearance left her with a very deep impression.

In his early days in Subei, Xiang Nan's clothes were a mixture of local and Western dress, in clear contrast to those of the soldiers around him. This is the earliest surviving picture of Xiang after his arrival in Subei. He had exceptional linguistic talents. Soon after reaching Subei, he could speak the local dialect like a native, something that amazed his colleagues

The group of young girl students, led by Wang Zhixin, went to report to the county government office. Lo and behold, the government secretary there who received their report was none other than the young cadre Wang had observed earlier in the morning. After Xiang Nan familiarised himself with their backgrounds, he looked at Wang Zhixin's fine written script and saw the calm and competent young woman making her report, and promptly fell in love.

The other students were quickly dispatched elsewhere. Only Wang Zhixin remained behind.

Xiang Nan told Wang that she would be assigned to the newly established ninth district to do propaganda work. He introduced her in detail to the situation in this district and learned more from Wang Zhixin about conditions in the anti-Japan school.

In 1944, Xiang Nan (in a white shirt, standing second from right) led a group of workers in a struggle against landlords and capitalists to protect the workers' rights. In Fudong county, they established the Dongkan city general labour union

At that point, Wang Zhixin only figured that Secretary Xiang seemed youthful, warm hearted and sincere, so she liked him well enough.

Wang Zhixin didn't realise until a few days later, when she encountered Xiang Nan carrying her effects, that Xiang Nan was the newly named party secretary for the ninth district. Once they were in love, Xiang Nan 'made a full confession' that, once he had learned that he was being sent to the ninth district, he had managed to arrange for Wang Zhixin to be sent there, too.

Born in 1916, Wang Zhixin was two years older than Xiang Nan. But as they worked together, Xiang Nan adopted a protective, elder brother attitude towards her.

Though Xiang Nan was young, he had seen a lot. His background was rich with experience, and he had come to know many places. The stories he told came to life and were compelling. Wang Zhixin told Xiang Nan about her own hard life as well.

Wang Zhixin was born in Fenghua county, Zhejiang province. From the time she was small, she went with her father as he tried to earn a living on a shoestring. After that, she found work in a cotton mill, struggling to earn money to help her family. She studied on her own, and managed to complete her middle school education by going to night school. Then she became a teacher in a primary school. Around that time, she embraced the idea of communism. With the outbreak of war with Japan, Wang Zhixin left Shanghai for the New Fourth Army area, where she became part of a detachment of girl students in the No. 5 branch school affiliated with the 'Resist Japan University'.

Wang Zhixin (front row, second from right) with fellow students at the No. 5 branch school of the 'Resist Japan University'

The love between Xiang Nan and Wang Zhixin would soon be tested in the fires of war.

Yanfu district was the very heart of the anti-Japanese base area in Subei. The New Fourth Army's third division, part of its main battle force, and New Forth Army headquarters, were both located there. In the first days of February 1943, two Japanese divisions and 20,000 puppet troops advanced from Xuzhou and Huaiyin to carry out a 'mopping-up operation' against Yanfu. The New Fourth Army had early warning of the assault; when the combined force of Japanese and puppet troops failed to achieve their goal, they divided into several columns to execute a 'sift and clean-up' operation, inflicting heavy destruction on the anti-Japanese base area. Xiang Nan, transferred to be party secretary in the ninth district, led the party committee cadres and the populace in strengthening the area's defensive works, so as to blunt the enemy's clean-up operations, while at the same time waiting for opportunities to pick off small groups of enemy soldiers on the move, interfering with the Japanese and puppet forces' 'mopping-up' campaign.

In those harsh days of the 'mopping-up' campaign, Xiang Nan and Wang Zhixin encountered each other from dawn to dusk, and their love rapidly bloomed. Once the struggle against the enemy's mopping-up campaign was over, conditions in the Yanfu base region gradually settled down. Early in 1944, Xiang Nan and Wang Zhixin informed their higher-level commanders that they wanted to marry. What neither of them anticipated was that the organisation would turn them down. The reason was simple: marrying was not in accord with the '285' rule.

According to this rule, at least one party cadre in a couple who wanted to marry had to be at least 28 years old and to have been a party member for at least five years, or else hold positions at deputy regiment level or above. Xiang Nan and Wang Zhixin had fulfilled only two of these three requirements: Wang was 28, and Xiang Nan, who had joined the party in 1938, had more than five years' membership.

Xiang Nan (second from right front row), Wang Zhixin (second row, third from right) and fighting comrades at the Fudong anti-Japan base, 1944

Xiang Nan and Wang Zhixin married nonetheless. In the thatched hut of a peasant family they held a simple wedding ceremony. Some military comrades and a few of Wang Zhixin's schoolmates heard the news and came to offer their congratulations, and the little courtyard soon filled with the noisy sounds of celebration.

In 1944, Xiang Nan and his wife welcomed the birth of their first child. Although conditions in the base area at the time were extremely harsh, the party organisation permitted the provision of milk powder and sugar to the infant offspring of the married couple. The marriage of Xiang Nan and Wang Zhixin had not received party approval, and thus did not merit this special treatment. When Xiang Nan saw that the baby was soon to be born, he prepared a carton containing some cotton clothing, eggs and other items, and sent it to the local military medical station. He also sought out a village woman named Qiu and arranged for her to take care of the baby in her home.

In that bitter wartime environment, nutrition was desperately lacking. Wang Zhixin became very weak, and her weight dropped to a mere 36 kilograms. To find better nutrition for his wife and their child, Xiang Nan would stand by the banks of the frozen river in winter, watching his countrymen catching fish. Then, from his meagre pay, he would buy tiny fish from the fishermen, bring them home and make a broth for Wang Zhixin.

When the baby was a month old, Xiang Nan and Wang Zhixin, braving the icy wind and stumbling through deep snow, went off to their district party committee to take part in 'rectification movement' study sessions. During the party rectification campaign in Subei, Xiang Nan had some very difficult moments. He never disclosed clearly his father's political leanings. His marriage to Wang Zhixin had never been approved by the party organisation, which was a violation of party discipline. With respect to the first item in particular, because he refused to go into detail about his father's occupation, once the rectification campaign was over, his comrades continued to believe that the father's history was definitely a problem, and they set out to 'educate' Xiang Nan, insisting over and over that he clarify all before the party's organisation department. Later, one leader of the rectification campaign finally put an end to this, saying: "This matter is over. Let's worry about it some later." And with that, Xiang Nan was finally exonerated.

Chapter 7

'If That Bridge is Not Up and Running by Nightfall, I Will Have You Shot'

Japan surrendered unconditionally on 15 August 1945. By that time, the four liberated zones of Huainan (meaning south of the Huai river), Huaibei (north of the Huai river), Suzhong (central Jiangsu) and Subei (northern Jiangsu) had joined together in a single belt to become a large, liberated region of more than 30m people.

Central party authorities decided on a policy of 'expanding to the north while guarding the south'. The third division of the New Fourth Army, numbering 30,000, was transferred to northeastern China from its original bases in the Yan-Huai area in northern Jiangsu. The remaining 80,000 troops of the New Fourth Army were shifted north to Shandong province. In this period, Xiang Nan departed Fudong, with successive assignments as a construction section chief in the fifth and 11th special administrative districts within Subei, and as chief of various economic and financial departments.

Xiang Nan in Subei, 1946

With the breakdown of negotiations between the KMT and the CPC, the situation in the two Huai river liberated zones that lay close to the KMT's political headquarters in Nanjing became extremely serious. When KMT forces launched a major offensive against the Subei liberated zone, the CPC central China bureau decided to withdraw from the liberated zones south and north of the Huai river.

'If That Bridge is Not Up and Running by Nightfall, I Will Have You Shot'

Xiang Nan, Wang Zhixin and their eldest son Xiang Xiaohong in Subei, 1947

Deng Zihui, who headed the central China bureau, was worried the most by the logistical problems behind the front lines. A fast army was gathering and moving to the north, but logistics behind them were chaotic. Deng Zihuei assigned responsibility to Liu Ruilong with orders to get the logistical situation in the rear under control at any cost. Xiang Nan, ready to serve any mission at this critical juncture, was transferred to the logistics command in Subei as chief of supplies.

No sooner had Xiang Nan taken up his new duties than he was plunged into battle at Lianshui, in northern Jiangsu. This was a ferocious hand-to-hand struggle between the communist central China field army and the crack 74th KMT division. In charge of the unit tasked with mobilising the resources of the local populace, Xiang Nan was responsible for a bridge that crossed the river. The bridge was relatively new, and had been bombed by the enemy. Waiting on one bank of the river were the personnel of the agencies trying to move northward, and cadres' families; troops headed southward waited impatiently on the opposite bank.

Xiang Nan immediately ordered labourers drawn from the local populace to start building a bridge. Just then, a messenger arrived with word from

Tan Zhenlin, the deputy political commissar for the central China region: "If that bridge is not up and running by nightfall, I will have you shot!"

Armies are not in the habit of making operatic speeches. Xiang Nan knew this was utterly serious. The entire battle hung on whether he could erect a functional bridge in time. What a shame that the bridge built with so much effort and hardship had been demolished, causing the chaotic situation he now confronted. In the conflagration of battle, no excuses for failing to build the bridge could be tolerated. He ordered the men under his command to redouble their efforts, and by nightfall they managed to erect a temporary bridge. Tan Zhenlin brought a column of troops from his military headquarters down to the riverbank. Finding that the civilian personnel and military units had all smoothly crossed the river under Xiang Nan's direction, Tan heaped public praise on him. Xiang Nan's exceptional ability to mobilise and organise people left Tan Zhenlin with a very deep impression.

On a 1983 visit with a Fujian delegation, Xiang Nan (front row, third from right) and Han Peixin, Jiangsu party secretary (front row, fourth from right) visit the New Fourth Army revolutionary exhibition in Yancheng, Jiangsu

In 1996, beginning his recovery, Xiang Nan moved from the Beijing Hospital to his family home. Some of Xiang Nan's wartime comrades made a special trip from Nanjing to see him in hospital in Beijing. In the front row, third from left is Hu Wei, head of the rectification campaign team of the time. Far left is the wife of Hu Wei. In the rear, second from left is Wang Zhixin. First and second on the right are Ding Zhaojia and his wife

In the 1990s, Xiang Nan and Wang Zhixin returned to Subei to view the New Fourth Army commemorative hall in Yancheng

Chapter 8

Entering the Youth League Apparatus

On 1 January 1949, the central party authorities formally announced the establishment of the China New Democracy Youth League. All central party organisations quickly selected groups of young cadres from across country to come to Beijing for the league's first national congress.

Tan Zhenlin, who was then the deputy political commissar of the Third Field Army, instantly thought of Xiang Nan.

Xiang Nan, Huang Xinbai, Wang Huadong and Liu Xing, representing the Anhui Youth League, on a visit to Beijing for the first national congress of the China New Democracy Youth League. This photo shows Xiang Nan (far left) and his comrades after arriving in Beijing in March 1949

Xiang Nan (left) with Huang Xinbai (centre) in Beijing while attending the first congress of the China New Democracy Youth League, April 1949

At that time, Xiang Nan was working in his new post as head of the propaganda department of the party committee in the Jiangsu-Huai river region. When he received his new orders, he hurried through the night to Hefei and reported to Zeng Xisheng, secretary of the north Anhui district party committee. Zeng said to Xiang Nan: "You are instructed to go to the first youth league congress in Beijing, by order of Tan Zhenlin."

Along with Huang Xinbai, Wang Huadong and Liu Xing, who had been chosen by the north Anhui party committee, Xiang Nan travelled north in fits and starts by rail from Bengbu along the Jinpu line, finally reaching Beijing after nearly a week.

The first national congress of the China New Democracy Youth League lasted eight days. Chairman Mao Zedong and Commander-in-Chief Zhu De visited the young delegates to the congress at the Fragrant Hills Shuangqing retreat outside Beijing on 24 April 1949.

On 24 April 1949, CPC Chairman Mao Zedong, along with Central Secretariat Secretary and PLA Commander-in-Chief Zhu De, received a group of delegates to the first congress of the China New Democracy Youth League at the Shuangqing retreat in Beijing. Xiang Nan took photos of Mao and Zhu with his own camera, and treasured these photos throughout his lifetime

The first congress of the China New Democracy Youth League convenes in Beijing, April 1949

Xiang Nan (right) and Huang Xinbai (centre) tour the Forbidden City during the congress

In November 1951, Xiang Nan attended the second plenary session of the central committee of the China New Democracy Youth League, warmly received by Mao Zedong, Zhu De, and party and state leaders

Returning from Beijing to northern Anhui, Xiang Nan and his group made their report to Zeng Xisheng. Zeng ordered them to organise a northern Anhui New Democracy Youth League congress right away, and the four of them remained involved in youth league work in northern Anhui.

Ever since he had started putting out anti-Japanese information, Xiang Nan had maintained his spirit of youthful enthusiasm and vigour. No matter where he went, he was always able reach into the hearts of young soldiers and cadres, whether through singing, theatrical performances or other forms of entertainment. The melodies Xiang Nan played on his harmonica stayed with the soldiers when they rested between battles, bringing contentment to all.

Under Xiang Nan's leadership, the first congress of the Northern Anhui Youth League and the first northern Anhui student congress promptly convened. A Northern Anhui Youth League school opened as well, for the training of a substantial core of youth league members.

Entering the Youth League Apparatus

Xiang Nan was a person who loved beauty. When he was at primary school, he adored planting in the garden and beautifying his environment. Wherever he went, he left botanical beauty behind. Because they had no place to live, some of the young people in the youth league's provincial committee bodies had no choice but to find shelter in spartan grass huts on the outskirts of the city. Xiang Nan saw how dismal their conditions were, and persuaded them to take their problems in their own hands. Soon, they built the 'home of youth', with little bridges over bubbling waters, flowers and grasses in profusion and, in springtime, the red flowers of plum trees and the brilliant green of willows. This soothed the hearts of the young people, and soon the young cadres still living inside the city were competing to move out to this peaceful home.

Xiang Nan is second from right in the third row of this enlarged section of the group photo

One winter evening in 1949, when Xiang Nan was in his office working overtime on some documents, he received a phone call from Wu Guang, who was then the head of the provincial office of the All-China Women's Federation. She told Xiang Nan that Qian Zhengying, Huang Xinbai's fiancée, was about to arrive. Xiang Nan hurried to find Huang Xinbai. Xiang Nan was overjoyed for his wartime comrade, and he quickly wrote a message for his communications orderly to carry to Huang.

When Xiang Nan entered the room of the orderly, he found the man sound asleep. He did not have the heart to awaken the sleeping youth, so he himself waded several miles through deep snow to find Huang Xinbai and send him rushing off to the women's federation in search of Wu Guang. Huang Xinbai had no idea what was happening, and was still daydreaming. Xiang Nan stuffed the paper into his hand, saying: "You had better get going!"

What was written on the paper were these words: "Amid the snowy vastness, Qian is coming. Hurry!"

At the first northern Anhui student congress

The first northern Anhui youth congress convenes in Hefei, November 1949

Xiang Nan (left) with a model youth at the first northern Anhui youth congress, November 1949

During his leadership of the Northern Anhui Youth League, Xiang Nan convened the first northern Anhui youth congress, the first northern Anhui student congress and opened the northern Anhui youth league school to train large numbers of youth league members

In the summer of 1949, young delegates to the northern Anhui youth league congress organised young shock brigades to perform voluntary labour. Xiang Nan speaks to the young delegates before they head for their volunteer work

Entering the Youth League Apparatus

Xiang Nan (left) and young cadres take a break at a volunteer labour site

Xiang Nan in the courtyard of the youth league's Anhui provincial committee

Xiang Nan (centre) and Wang Zhixin (left) during Xiang's work with the youth league's Anhui provincial committee

Xiang Nan (left) and Huang Xinbai (right) lead youth league volunteer labour

Chapter 9

Xiang Nan Finds Xiang Nan

In 1951, the north Anhui and south Anhui working committees of the youth league merged, creating the Anhui provincial working committee of the China New Democracy Youth League. Xiang Nan became secretary, while also serving as secretary of the Communist Party committee of Anhui University.

One day, at a meeting of the provincial party committee, Party Secretary Zeng Xisheng gave Xiang Nan a new assignment, asking his help in finding the missing son of an old wartime comrade. The wartime comrade's name was Liang, and he had been working in the northeast. Someone told him that his missing son was working with the youth league in Anhui, so he had written to Zeng Xisheng to ask for help in his search.

Xiang Nan (standing, fourth from left) with colleagues at Anhui University, 1951

Soon after that, Zeng ran into Xiang Nan at a meeting and asked whether Xiang Nan had been able to help find the son of his comrade. Xiang Nan replied that he had not seen the boy; there were more than 100,000 members in the north Anhui youth league, and plenty of them were named Liang. He had searched at length but had found nothing.

Zeng Xisheng quickly showed his disappointment, answering: "If I saw this comrade's boy, I would probably recognise him, because when the boy was little, he lived in Shanghai, on Rue Vouillement."

Xiang Nan responded: "I lived in Shanghai on the very same street."

Zeng Xisheng was amazed. "What was your street address on Rue Vouillement?" he asked.

Xiang Nan told him the number affixed to the entry gate of his home there.

Zeng carefully looked Xiang Nan up and down, and asked: "Do you remember seeing an older fellow with a beard?"

Xiang Nan replied: "Of course I saw him. He used to take me to the movies."

Zeng Xisheng said: "Look at me. Do you know who I am?"

Xiang Nan peered closely at Zeng, stupefied.

The world is full of coincidences. Zeng Xisheng was formerly none other than the "bearded older fellow", and Xiang Nan was the boy he had taken to the cinema.

Zeng Xisheng's wartime comrade was Xiang Nan's father, Xiang Yunian, who changed his name to Liang Mingde after he left Shanghai. With that change of name, where could anyone have found 'Liang Mingde's boy'?

Thus, Xiang Nan found Xiang Nan.

But for the sake of his work, Xiang Nan could only hide for the time being his longing to see his father again, silently waiting for the day when they could be reunited.

Chapter 10

Reunited with his Long-lost Mother

Xiang Nan's work with the Anhui youth league went extremely well. His documents and reports showed clarity of perspective, clear organisation and, more generally, an ability to introduce new ways of looking at the work of the youth league. All of this brought him favourably to the attention of the central leadership of the youth league and the leaders of the party's east China bureau.

Xiang Nan (front row, fourth from left) with comrades at the fifth plenary meeting of the east China working committee of the youth league, April 1953

Xiang Nan: Champion of Reform in Fujian

Xiang Nan with his wife and his mother and father in Beijing, 1955

Xiang Nan (left), Wang Xhixin (third from left) and colleagues from the east China working committee of the youth league in Qingdao, 1954

Xiang Nan (second from left) and colleagues from the party's east China bureau working committee, on Dongping Road in Shanghai, 1954

Xiang Nan (third from left, second row) with youth league cadres while on an investigation visit to the grassroot

Reunited with his Long-lost Mother

Xiang Nan and Wang Zhixin in Shanghai

Xiang Nan's six children, photographed in Shanghai, 1955

In the second half of 1952, Xiang was named second party secretary in the east China bureau of the China Youth League. He did not formally take up the job, however, until early 1953. Wang Zhixin also moved to Shanghai, to become deputy head of the youth work department of the league's east China bureau.

Xiang Nan and Wang Zhixin had both spent their youth in Shanghai, and they had especially warm and familiar feelings for this city. Most important of all, Xiang Nan was able to reunite with his mother, of whom he had lost track for many years.

After the new China was established in 1949, Xiang Nan sent people in search of news of his mother, and wrote letters to people in his home village, trying to find out what had happened to her, but no reliable information came to him. The party centre dispatched teams on missions of sympathy to western Fujian, where they posted lists of missing persons. From this, Xiang Nan was overjoyed to be able to discover his mother's name. He sent an emissary to bring his mother to Shanghai.

After spending some time locked away in Shanghai's Tilanqiao prison, Xiang Nan's mother was able to leave the prison with the help of comrades from the party underground, and she brought her young daughter back to their home village. Her daughter had contracted an illness while in prison,

Reunited with his Long-lost Mother

In the 1950s, Xiang Nan often took his children to the park on holidays. He kept many photos from those days, revealing the warmth and happiness of his family life

and died shortly after she and her mother reached home. Alone after her daughter's death, the woman's heart yearned constantly for her boy, and on the eve of the revolution she was wandering through the old family areas in western Fujian seeking her loved one. In 1950, Xie Juezai, the distinguished legal educator and newly appointed minister of internal affairs, led a team of central party representatives to western Fujian on a mission of sympathy, searching for elderly relatives and local friends of those who fought in the revolution. They compiled registers of names, and placed advertisements in local newspapers. In the end, that is how Xiang Nan and his mother were finally reunited.

His mother's arrival added to the joy and contentment of Xiang Nan's household. At about this time, Xiang Nan and his wife welcomed their sixth child, and his mother took on all the duties of caring for the children. Xiang Nan and Wang Zhixin threw all their energies into their work.

Xiang Nan with his son, Xiang Xiaolan, at Beidaihe

Chapter 11

A First Foreign Visit to the USSR

After his appointment to the working committee of the east China bureau of the youth league, Xiang Nan immediately took part in preparations for the second youth league congress, to be held in Shanghai. Compared with the work he had done in Anhui, this work in Shanghai seemed sluggish. The first congress of the Shanghai new democratic youth league had convened only in 1953. After Xiang Nan took his position, the east China bureau working committee decided to hold a second congress of the Shanghai youth league, only 11 months after the first one. At the second congress, Xiang Nan presented an address entitled 'The youth league must lead the way for all youth to study and uphold the general line of the party in this transitional period'.

In 1954, as party secretary to the working committee of the east China bureau of the youth league, Xiang Nan accompanied a youth league delegation to the USSR, to participate in the 12th congress of the USSR youth league

Xiang Nan with fellow delegate, Lu Jindong, at the Kremlin during his mission to the USSR in 1954

During his tenure with the east China working committee, Xiang Nan had the opportunity to meet with Alexander Shelepin, the party secretary and leading official of the Soviet youth league, accompanying him on his visit to Shanghai. The latter said with some conceit: "If you don't read Shakespeare, you're not doing the work of the youth league." He outlined his ideas on the influence that great art and literature played in affecting people's sentiments. Shelepin's wide-ranging remarks left a deep impression on Xiang Nan.

Fundamentally, Xiang was a person who loved to read and learn, whether he was involved in anti-Japanese national salvation operations in Fujian or working at the grassroots in rural Subei. He always had a book with him. But conditions were difficult, and libraries were utterly lacking, so he simply read whatever book came to hand. One might be *A History of the Soviet Communist Party (Bolshevik)*. Another might be a mouldy copy of *The Romance of the Three Kingdoms*, or *All Men Are Brothers*, or other such famous tales, bound in traditional Chinese style, which he browsed through in the house of one of his landlord's neighbours. Once he reached the more favourable environment of Shanghai, Xiang Nan could borrow all sorts of books from the city's libraries, something that gave him great pleasure. When he was not working, Xiang Nan spent most of his time reading. He grew familiar with many well-known authors worldwide, including, of course, *The Collected Works of William Shakespeare*, as recommended by Alexander Shelepin, and delved into many works of philosophy and economics.

The front cover of Xiang Nan's *Diary of a Visit to the USSR*

In March 1954, as a member of a China youth league delegation, Xiang Nan travelled to Moscow to take part in the 12th congress of the Soviet youth league.

This was Xiang Nan's first trip abroad, and it left him with deep impressions of the USSR. Xiang Nan was filled with respect for the world's first socialist nation. When he returned to China, he published the diary of his visit to the USSR in serial form in the Shanghai newspapers *Youth News* and *China Youth Daily*. On his publisher's recommendation, Xiang Nan also re-worked his diary and published it in book form as *A Diary of a Visit to the USSR*. Some 20,000 copies were published. Amazingly, at the same time that Xiang Nan was praising Soviet socialist construction to the skies, he was becoming acutely aware of existing problems in economic construction there. He offered some examples: "In department stores, daily necessities such as cotton cloth and pharmaceuticals and books are extremely cheap, but a shirt of decent quality can cost 200 roubles. On a product-for-product basis, one could buy a small car for the price of only

Part of Xiang Nan's *Diary of a Visit to the USSR*, published by Shanghai People's Publishing House in 1955

30 shirts. Such a conversion is not terribly meaningful, but it does show that some light industrial products in the Soviet Union are very expensive, while a number of heavy industrial products are as cheap as they are."

In September 1954, as an elected delegate from Anhui province, Xiang Nan attended the first national people's congress (NPC) to be held in the new China. He was among the youngest of the 1,226 delegates to the congress. For Xiang Nan, this was a milestone in his life. Shortly after the NPC adjourned, Xiang Nan bade farewell to Shanghai.

In 1954, Xiang Nan was elected as a representative of Anhui province to the NPC. This is a group photo of the Anhui delegation, taken during the first NPC in Beijing. In the front row, second from left is Zhang Bojun; third from left is Zhu Yunshan; fifth from left is Zeng Xisheng; eighth from left is Fang Lingru; 10th from left is Li Jinxi; 11th from left is Li Da; 12th from left is Zhou Gengsheng; 13th from left is Huang Yan. In the second row, third from left is Zhang Jingfu; fourth from left is Mei Ru; sixth from left is Li Kenong, 10th from left is Zhao Puchu. In the third row, far left is Xiang Nan; seventh from left is Sun Qimeng

Chapter 12

A Capable Assistant to Hu Yaobang, Top Leader of the Youth League

In February 1955, Xiang Nan was transferred to Beijing to become the chief of the central-level propaganda department of the youth league. Xiang was 37, and the first secretary of the youth league, Hu Yaobang, was only 40.

In May 1955, Xiang Nan (front row, seventh from right) accompanied the first secretary of the youth league, Hu Yaobang (front row, eighth from right), on a visit to northeast China, and sat for this photograph with comrades from Jilin province youth league

After Hu Yaobang's quick elevation to the top position in the youth league, he set about convening the third central committee of the first congress of the youth league. Mao Zedong personally delivered a speech, raising two issues for the league. The first issue was how the party committee would provide it with leadership. The second was what sort of work the youth league should carry out. These two matters engaged the thinking of Hu Yaobang and leading cadres of the youth league at all levels.

Xiang Nan (front, sixth from right) and Hu Yaobang (front, fifth from right) on a visit to the First Auto Works in Changchun city, Jilin province, May 1956

Beginning in the spring of 1955, after Mao Zedong raised these two matters, Xiang Nan carried out a number of research investigations and published an insightful article in *China Youth Daily* after Hu Yaobang himself had read it. This article was regarded as among the best of its genre, and made a strong impression on Hu Yaobang.

At that time, the leadership stratum of the youth league was young and full of energy. Hu Yaobang, well aware of the importance of publicity, took a careful interest in the selection of the central publicity section chief. For his part, Xiang Nan was living up to Hu Yaobang's high expectations, and quickly mastered the requirements of his new assignment.

Xiang Nan was very happy with Hu Yaobang's democratic and easygoing work style. He participated in the drafting of the youth league leadership's important documents and discussion on major issues of policy and strategic direction. Wherever Hu Yaobang travelled around the country, Xiang Nan was like a shadow beside him.

Xiang Nan was not a man of many words, but when he spoke he was often very humorous, and his comrades developed a feeling of real closeness to him. He regularly went to various offices, factories or mines to make reports, usually writing them up in his own hand. He enjoined his young audiences to play distinctive roles in production and national reconstruction, and to do battle with bureaucratism and other unhealthy practices, but at the same time he took great interest in the healthy growth of young people, exhorting them to adhere to high ideals and a correct outlook on life. At a time when people, young and old, male and female, were wearing the same blue cotton clothing, leading some foreigners to call them 'blue ants', Xiang Nan called for establishing a 'committee to improve our clothing', and suggested that members of the youth league wear multicoloured clothes.

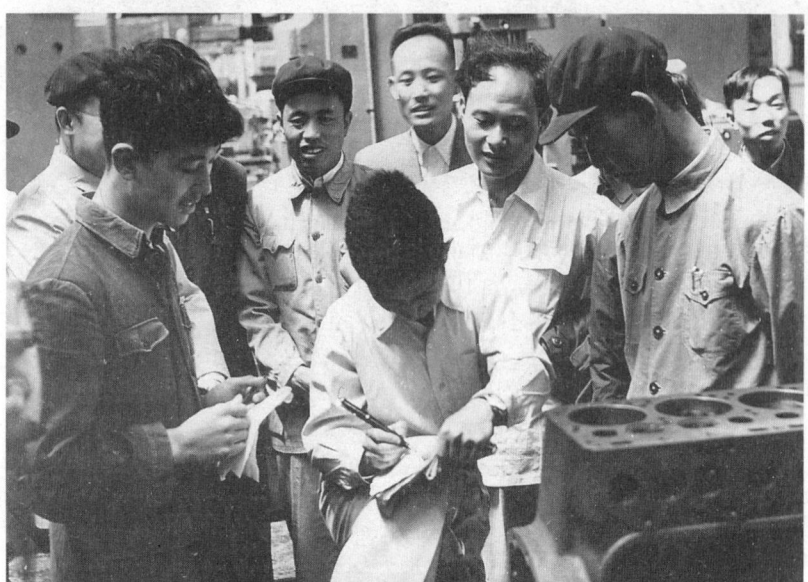

Xiang Nan (front row, second from right) and Hu Yaobang (front row, third from right) visit the First Auto Works in Changchun. Hu writes a message for young workers

With Hu Yaobang's endorsement, Xiang Nan started a movement for 'youths advance towards science', with great fanfare. With the support of the senior league leadership and a cover inscription by Zhou Enlai, the magazine *Knowledge Is Power*, which aimed to popularise scientific understanding, was warmly received. The league's leadership also organised visits by league members to top-ranked scientists such as Hua Luogeng, Li Siguang and Zhu Kezhen, urging the young people to follow in the great scientists' footsteps. To encourage young people's artistic and literary creation, under Xiang Nan's guidance, the central leadership of the league and the all-China writers' association convened a national young writers' creative works conference.

In the gigantic movement to eliminate illiteracy, the top leadership of the youth league decided to put 30m literate young people to the task of eliminating illiteracy among 70m rural dwellers. Xiang Nan viewed this decision with great seriousness. Every year, he organised 'youth brigades against illiteracy', study classes that earned work points and winter studies for peasants in the agricultural off season, turning literate young people into young teachers, writing literacy text books in community after community, and giving practical reality to the youth league leaders' movement to combat illiteracy. Mao Zedong, in his *High Tide of Socialism in the Chinese Countryside*, affirmed the experiences of the youth league's anti-illiteracy campaign in the village of Gaojialiugou, in Junan county, Shandong province. Xiang Nan put this model to work widely. After Hu Yaobang reported on it to Mao Zedong, it won Mao's high praise and was then extended nationwide.

Chapter 13

Reuniting with his Father in Shenyang

Xiang Nan and his father Xiang Yunian managed to make contact in 1951, and remained in touch during those years. Finally, in 1955, Xiang Nan and Wang Zhixin took advantage of a trip to Beijing for a conference, and went up to Shenyang to see Xiang's father. After 21 years, father and son were reunited in Shenyang.

After he reached Yan'an, Xiang Yunian had changed his name to Liang Mingde. In 1955, he was serving as deputy head of the Liaoning provincial procuracy office. At the time of their parting, Xiang Nan was still young and inexperienced. Twenty-one years later, at their meeting, he was a youthful leader of the youth league. Xiang Yunian's happiness was beyond words. But face to face with the man he knew so well but whose appearance was so unfamiliar, his heartfelt words swelled up from the depths.

Xiang Yunian in Shenyang, 1955

After completing the Long March with the central Red Army, Xiang Yunian took on a new assignment – building the party's underground operations in KMT-controlled areas. After the formation of the second KMT-CPC united front in 1937, the party sent him to study at the central party school in Yan'an. During the war of resistance, Xiang Yunian served as the

Xiang Nan (left) and Xiang Yunian (right) reunited in Shenyang after 21 years of separation, spring 1955

head of united front departments in the central plains region of Shaanxi province and in Suide, Shaanxi province. In the ensuing civil war, he was involved in building the communist forces' northeast China base, first in Songjiang province (which later became part of Heilongjiang province) and then in Liaoning province. Xiang Yunian himself glossed over his years of underground struggle in a sentence or two. Even to his son, who was already a high-ranking party cadre, when it came to party secrets, Xiang Yunian's lips were sealed.

One matter could not be avoided when father and son got together again. In Yan'an, Xiang Yunian had married a comrade named Wu Jian, and had formed another family. When Xiang Nan and his wife came to Shenyang to see Xiang Nan's father, Wu Jian was very anxious. She even offered to withdraw, to help Xiang Yunian's family reunion.

Xiang Nan, his wife and Xiang Yunian at the northern tombs in Shenyang, 1955. On the right in the first row is Xiang Xiaoqing. Next to her is Xiang Xiaobai

Xiang Nan's father Xiang Yunian and his mother Wang Cunyu with their grandchildren in Tiananmen Square on China's national day holiday, 1955

Xiang Yunian in Beijing, 1956

Xiang Nan felt very awkward as well. He had found his mother and now his father. It would be hard to see them together. What child does not dream that his own parents' broken marriage might be restored? But in the years of war, his father's relationship with Wu Jian deserved no criticism. Xiang Nan was not someone who clung to the old ways, but he found it hard to discuss any of this with his father.

It was Wang Zhixin who finally resolved this extremely difficult situation. Wang Zhixin and Wu Jian took to each other like old friends. They were just about the same age, and their backgrounds were similar. Though this was their first meeting, they had plenty to talk about. Her father-in-law Xiang Yunian, though, remained reserved and quiet.

Wang Zhixin criticised Xiang Yunan for not fulfilling his responsibilities to his family and his wife Wang Cunyu. Xiang Yunian frankly admitted his failings. Wang Zhixin said to her father-in-law: "Now you have a new family. Xiang Nan and I are not opposed to it."

She told him that Xiang Nan's mother, Wang Cunyu, was living with them, and would never try to seek out Xiang Yunian in the future. But Wang Zhixin told Xiang Yunian that she hoped he would not proceed with a formal divorce, to protect Wang Cunyu's feelings. If an opportunity came along, Wang Zhixin told Xiang Yunian, he should pay a visit to Xiang Nan's mother.

Xiang Nan and his father in Guangzhou, 1958

Xiang Yunian at Yulin, on the island of Hainan, 1960

Xiang Nan and his wife visit commemorative sites of his father's wartime service in Suide, Shaanxi province, in the 1990s

On this trip to Shenyang, Xiang Nan and his wife brought along their daughter Xiang Xiaoqing and their second son Xiang Xiaobai. This was the children's first long train trip, and they could hardly control their excitement and curiosity. They did not understand the bigger personal matters going on around them, but they were a little intimidated by the old gentleman who was even taller than their father.

Before the visit ended, Xiang Yunian joined Xiang Nan and his family on a visit to the northern tombs in Shenyang, and they had a look around the city. Amid the chill of early springtime, their hearts were warmed by their family feelings, their smiles as bright as the rays of the sun.

Chapter 14

Luckily Escaping the Misfortune of Being Branded a Rightist

The third congress of the China new democracy youth league took place in Beijing between 5 May and 25 May 1957, attended by 1,493 delegates. By this time, the youth league had 23m members nationwide, with 92,000 league organisations at the grassroots level. At this congress, Hu Yaobang was elected first secretary of the youth league, and Xiang Nan was elected as secretary of the youth league secretariat.

While the youth league congress was in session, the central party leadership issued a document on 4 May entitled *Instructions of the Central Party Leadership Regarding Ongoing Attempts to Organise Personages*

Mao Zedong and Liu Shaoqi welcome delegates to the third youth league, 1957

In May 1957, the China new democracy youth league changed its name to the China young communist league. The photo, taken at the third national congress of the young communist league, shows league members presenting flowers to the presidium (Xiang Nan is fifth from left in the second row). At the first session of the standing committee of this congress, Xiang Nan was elected secretary of the central secretariat of the youth league

Outside the Party to Criticise the Party's Mistakes and Shortcomings; another document entitled *Matters are Undergoing Great Changes* was issued on 15 May, and on 16 May yet another, entitled *Instructions of the Central Party Leadership on Dealing With Criticisms by Non-party Personages*.

Immersed in the urgent business of convening the successful third youth league congress, it is not surprising that neither Hu Yaobang nor Xiang Nan gave too much thought to the possibility that the anti-rightist movement would have any connection to the work of the league. But these documents, directed to those working at provincial- and ministerial-level posts, led them to fear that a major political struggle was unfolding, and they consequently grew extremely cautious about saying anything.

China Youth Daily, published by the league's central leadership, was at this time extremely popular with young readers. Hu Yaobang issued a number of instructions on how to run the newspaper. In 1956, he proposed an overall approach of 'plenty of praise, plenty of criticism', which was strongly encouraging to the staff of the newspaper. With Hu's support, *China Youth Daily* produced a supplement called *Hot Pepper*, filled with satire and critical articles. The reading public gave it a very warm welcome.

Xiang Nan himself was not a key figure in running the newspaper, but whether in his capacity as head of the publicity department of the young communist league or as secretary to the league's party secretariat, he firmly supported further publication of critical article content. He had himself written more than a few essays aiming to puncture some of the ills of the time. But good times never last very long. Starting in the first half of 1957, criticism and accusations from the highest levels grew ever more frequent. Hu Yaobang, as the league's leader, as well as publicity department head Xiang Nan and Zhang Liqun, chief editor at *China Youth Daily*, came under extreme pressure. *Hot Pepper* grew less and less 'hot', until finally a reader sent a cartoon to the newspaper. A person buying food asks the foodseller: "Do you have any heatless hot peppers?" The seller replies: "Definitely! Just look for them in *China Youth Daily*!" Hot or not, it was already very difficult for Hu Yaobang to prevent the publication from being shut down.

Xiang Nan in May 1957, just after his election as secretary in the youth league central secretariat and his concurrent appointment as head of the league's central publicity department

Friendly organisations from various places in Japan welcome the young communist league delegation led by Xiang Nan, 1957

Xiang Nan addresses the welcoming session organised by various Japanese organisations

In 1957, Xiang Nan led a communist youth league delegation on a visit to various locations in Japan

Xiang Nan (third from left) at a social gathering with Japanese youth groups, 1957

In June 1957, invited by the league's Japanese counterpart organisation, the Japan youth and women's conference, Xiang Nan led a young communist league delegation to Japan for a 29-day tour. Right after that, on 28 July, Xiang Nan became deputy leader of the league, and travelled with Hu Yaobang and a youth league delegation to the Soviet Union for the global youth celebration. Over 45 days, they visited many of the USSR's republics.

On its way home from visiting the USSR, the delegation also went to Xinjiang for an inspection visit. This was at the very time in 1957 when the 'anti-rightist' movement was at its peak. Xiang Nan managed to be away from Beijing for three months, far from the churning political struggles. Perhaps this stroke of luck kept him from being attacked as a rightist in that fearsome movement.

During his visit to Japan in 1957, Xiang Nan visits a machine-building plant

Chapter 15

Attending the Sixth World Youth Friendship Festival

On 28 July 1957, the China democratic youth delegation, led by Hu Yaobang with Xiang Nan as deputy leader, set out for Moscow to participate in the sixth world peace and friendship festival for youth and student friends. The size of the delegation was unprecedented. It included progressive production workers from the industrial and agricultural sectors, young workers, and representatives from the democratic parties, the religious sector, arts and literature, minority nationalities and overseas

Xiang Nan (third from left) and Hu Yaobang (third from right), lead a delegation to the USSR, meeting with youth leaders from around the world

Xiang Nan (second from right) and Hu Yaobang (centre) in the Chinese embassy in Moscow. On the left is the Chinese ambassador to the USSR, Liu Xiao, August 1957

Chinese who had returned to China. There were three song and dance troupes, two Beijing opera troupes and one acrobatic team. One top of that, the delegation included 500 Chinese students studying in the Soviet Union. The total size of the delegation exceeded twelve hundred.

The visit to the Soviet Union lasted 45 days. Around 30,000 young people from throughout the world participated in this huge festival. In addition to joining the peace and friendship festival, the Chinese delegation carried out extensive exchanges with many organisations connected to the USSR communist youth league.

The Chinese group led by Hu Yaobang and Xiang Nan was one of the largest delegations from a country in the socialist bloc. They engaged in wide-ranging contacts and exchanges with the youth delegations from other countries.

Various western news services reported on the visiting Chinese delegation, and in China the internal publication *Reference News* reprinted a number of the western reports.

Attending the Sixth World Youth Friendship Festival

Xiang Nan and Hu Yaobang visit the USSR, 1957

Under cold war conditions, in which Sino-American relations were extremely strained, Hu Yaobang and Xiang Nan, with Wu Xueqian and other leaders of the Chinese youth delegation, vigorously made use of the platform provided by the world youth peace and friendship festival to spread the word about the new China, introducing its accomplishments to young people from all over the globe and conveying the message that the Chinese people loved peace and opposed war. By sowing the seeds of friendship among young people worldwide, they achieved major successes.

While participating in all types of activities at the festival in the USSR, Xiang Nan and Hu Yaobang also visited some of the Soviet socialist republics that comprised the Soviet Union. These included the Russian SSR, the Ukrainian SSR, the Georgian SSR and Kazakhstan. Touring a number of cities, they paid visits to factories and collective farms. After his return to China, Xiang Nan published *Impressions from my Second Trip to the USSR* in *China Youth Daily*, and he made a presentation to 4,000 youth league members on learning from the experiences of the Soviet Union.

Xiang Nan plays with a dolphin in the Black Sea coastal city of Sukhumi, 1957

Xiang in the coastal city of Sukhumi, August 1957

Chapter 16

Suddenly Face to Face With the 'Anti-Right Deviation' Storm

By the time Xiang Nan's delegation returned to China from the Soviet Union, it was already early September 1957. As soon as they reached Urumqi, in Xinjiang, Hu Yaobang made an urgent phone call to Luo Yi, who was managing the league's affairs in Beijing while Hu and Xiang were out of the country, to learn how the youth league was faring in the ongoing 'anti-rightist' movement. When Luo Yi told him that more than 100 members of the league's central administration had been targeted as rightists, Hu turned pale. He ordered Luo Yi to stop all work and await his return to Beijing for further discussions.

Xiang Nan and Hu Yaobang visit the Mogao grotto at Dunhuang, 1957

Xiang Nan (front row, fifth from left), Hu Yaobang (front row, fourth from left) with comrades from the Wuwei local party committee in Gansu province, the municipal party committee and the youth league party committee, September 1957

Hu Yaobang and Xiang Nan proceeded with a number of inspections in northwest China after leaving Xinjiang, and returned to Beijing in mid-September. As soon as they arrived in Beijing, they sensed the thickness of the political atmosphere.

Seventy-one people in the central administration of the China Youth League (CYL) had been branded as 'rightists'. Of the more than 100 people working at *China Youth Daily* alone, 17 were denounced, including the chief editor, the deputy editor and other key cadres on both the editorial and business sides. Figures who were extremely close to Xiang Nan, and whose work had regularly intersected with his own, such as Zhong Peizhang and Chen Mo, were attacked as 'rightists'. Even Zhang Liqun, the general editor, barely avoided denunciation as a 'rightist'. Hu Yaobang said time and again: "We are facing catastrophic losses."

Xiang Nan was chilled to the marrow. If something these comrades had said qualified them as 'rightists', Xiang Nan, in his many speeches and reports, had surely done even more. Among the leaders of most local CYL chapters and the highest central leaders of the league alike, Xiang Nan was known for speaking his mind without reservation. Now, for a while, Xiang Nan's words, whether during his working trips abroad or in his reports on his work with the CYL, became extremely cautious. In published articles he went through the motions of criticising rightists. But deep in his heart, Xiang Nan could not comprehend this 'anti-rightist' movement.

In 1958, all of China fell into the frenzy of the Great Leap Forward. The 'anti-rightist' content of all publications was replaced by propaganda about the 'general line', the Great Leap Forward, people's communes and so on. At just this time, an old incident resurfaced, and the political climate surrounding the CYL once again was filled with tension.

Late in May 1958, the secretary responsible for overseeing the CYL at the party's central secretariat convened a meeting with a number of top leaders of the league. As soon as Party Secretary Hu Yaobang and several members of the CYL secretariat arrived, this secretary demanded in a

Xiang Nan (front, second from right) and Hu Yaobang (front, third from left) with responsible comrades from local, town and county CYL committees in Zhangye, Gansu province, September 1957

stern voice: "The All-China Labour Federation has begun its anti-rightist criticisms, and has criticised Lai Ruoyu. Do you know what this is really all about?"

At this question from a party leader, everyone stared blankly, with no idea how to reply.

The secretary from the party centre answered his own question. "This is a question of the relationship between mass organisations and the party," he said. "Go and have a careful look to see if there is anyone like this fellow within the CYL."

Xiang Nan and Hu Yaobang on a visit to Lanzhou in September 1957

In the first half of 1958, during the third plenum of the CYL's third central committee, the leadership of the league had to follow the instructions they received from higher authorities, carrying out internal searches for 'rightist elements' and reporting back to the party centre. Someone brought up a document called *Ten Recommendations*, which Xiang Nan had drafted for the top leadership of the CYL prior to its third congress in 1956.

The CYL's third congress had been an extremely important occasion in its history. Intensive preparations had begun long in advance, in order to ensure that all went smoothly. Xiang Nan was serving as the head of the publicity section of the league's central leadership, and was Hu Yaobang's crucial wordsmith. For the purpose of drafting the key documents of the congress, Xiang Nan was always at Hu Yaobang's side, taking his meals and sleeping at Hu's own residence, No. 6, Fuqiang Hutong, Beijing.

Xiang Nan at Jiayuguan, 1957

When Mao Zedong made his appearance at the second congress of the youth league in June 1953, he had offered remarks entitled 'The Work of the Youth League Must Take into Account the Special Characteristics of Youth'. In his talk, Mao pointed out: "The question of the CYL's excessive independence from the party is a thing of the past. Today, the league's problem is that that it doesn't have enough independent work, not that it is too independent." Mao went on: "The league must act in line with the central working tasks of the party but, in doing so, it must have its own independent work based on the particular characteristics of youth. In my talk with central league comrades, I suggested two themes that they should explore. One was how the party should lead the work of the CYL. The other was how the league should go about its own work. Both of these themes raised the question of how best to give consideration to those special characteristics of young people. We hear from party organisations everywhere that they are pleased with the work of the CYL, and pleased that it chimes with the core elements of the work of the party itself. But now, something has arisen that is less satisfying: the CYL's work has still not adequately accommodated itself to the special characteristics of the young, and has not taken on a set of independent activities. The leading bodies of the party and the CYL must learn from the work of the top echelon of party leadership, remain adept at embracing the central tasks of the party, take youth's particular features under special consideration, and both organise and educate further the broad masses of our youth."

In preparing for the CYL's third congress, the top leadership of the league assigned Liang Buting and Xiang Nan, acting in the spirit of Mao's comments, to come up with a broad picture of the CYL's real situation and to present their concrete views and suggestions for improvement of its future work.

On 11 June 1958, during the third plenum of the third CYL central committee, senior party leaders including Mao Zedong, Liu Shaoqi, Zhou Enlai, Zhu De and Chen Yun all participated in a plenary session and sat for a commemorative photo. From left to right: Hu Yaobang, Deng Xiaoping, Chen Yun, Zhu De, Mao Zedong, Liu Shaoqi, Zhou Enlai, Lin Biao and Xiang Nan

Some months later, Liang Buting and Xiang Nan produced two speech drafts. Liang Buting's title was 'Looking to the League's Third Congress to Resolve Three Questions Relating to the League's Development'. Xiang Nan's draft was entitled 'Ten Opinions'. The key elements of these 10 opinions were as follows: "The CYL must have its own distinctive features, and must truly become the linkage connecting the party with young people... Broaden democratic life. To fulfil the task of enhancing the creativity and activism of our youth in building socialism, democracy must be broadened inside the CYL. We must implement an elective system truly from the bottom up, and expand free and lively debate... Establish youth activity centres... Broaden the powers of self-governance... Mass organisations should handle their affairs according to needs of young people on the scene and in accord with feasible conditions." In the 'Ten Opinions', Xiang Nan also proposed that the CYL be independently financed; that it move away from a system that combined total dependence on the state with disinterest in the management of its own internal affairs; that CYL fees be collected in a serious manner; that the league improve the management of its enterprises and enhance its structural efficiency, and so on.

In 1987, Xiang Nan paid a visit to Liang Buting, then party secretary in Shandong province, at Linqing in Shandong

Xiang Nan's 'Ten Opinions' were in the form of a draft statement for the central secretariat of the CYL. Originally, the designated spokesman for the CYL turned out to be not Xiang Nan but Luo Yi, from the league's central secretariat. Luo Yi, however, was on temporary assignment accompanying Vice-Premier Chen Yi to Tibet for the first Tibet youth congress, so Xiang Nan temporarily assumed the role of spokesman.

When the draft statements of Xiang Nan and Liang Buting were under consideration at the CYL's top leadership level, they received unanimous praise. When the standing committee of the CYL's Communist Party reviewed the drafts, it decided to send Xiang Nan's 'Ten Opinions' draft to the CPC's central secretariat on behalf of the CYL's own secretariat, and to distribute the 'Ten Opinions' through the CYL organisation at all levels nationwide in order to seek additional comments.

For a long time, this report received no response at all. Finally, Liang Buting, who was then in charge of the general office of the CYL, contacted a colleague in the general office of the party to try to find news about the document. This colleague told Liang Buting confidentially: "Old Kang [Kang Sheng] has seen the report. He said: 'This is a power play by the CYL directed at the party centre'."

Liang Buting was shocked when he heard this. At that moment, Hu Yaobang and Xiang Nan were on an inspection tour in the northeast, and he had no way of letting Hu Yaobang know what he had learned. On the one hand he was concerned over what Hu and Xiang Nan might say while on their travels, and on the other hand he waited restlessly for them to come back to Beijing.

As soon as Hu Yaobang returned to the capital, Liang Buting presented him with his work report. But after all, what Liang related was not a formal view transmitted from the central party leadership. So Hu Yaobang and Xiang Nan did not take the message too seriously.

Once some secretary in the central party secretariat had passed responsibility for 'seizing rightists' over to the central leadership in the CYL, some people inside the league's central organs began preparing materials for use in political criticism, but Xiang Nan was kept in the dark, and had no hint of what was going on.

The third plenum of the third CYL central committee opened on 2 June 1958, and took place in two phases. The first phase concentrated on the CYL's work experiences since the beginning of the Great Leap Forward and discussed the tasks facing the organisation, making various recommendations as to major objectives looking forward. The second phase, however, suddenly turned into a debate over the question of the party's absolute leadership of the CYL's work; in reality, it turned into a fully fledged criticism of Xiang Nan.

The 'Ten Opinions' that Xiang Nan had drafted and that had been sent both to the central party organisation and throughout the CYL's ranks was now blasted as an "anti-party, anti-socialist right-opportunist marching order for the youth movement", which "demanded personnel powers, financial powers, authority over all activities and the power to speak" from the party. The 'Ten Opinions', the criticism continued, "advocates removing the distinction between league members and non-members, and promotes democratisation and liberalism".

Normally, a plenum like this would conclude in a week; this plenum ran for 73 days.

The conference finally came out with a 'resolution on Xiang Nan's errors'. It announced Xiang's removal from all positions inside and outside the party, and a sentence of two additional years of party investigation and observation. Sharing these criticisms were Liang Buting, the chief of the CYL's party secretariat, who was also subjected to precautionary measures and stripped of his duties in the secretariat.

Those days were the hardest in Xiang Nan's lifetime. He was born to a red family. He entered the party as a youth. He was loyal and devoted to the party. He had never dreamed that he might become a 'rightist element'.

During those days when he was subjected to criticism, Xiang Nan and his wife Wang Zhixin lived with constant uneasiness, often passing whole nights with no sleep. Yesterday, someone might have been their close friend and comrade, sharing joint tasks with them; then, a night later, that person might become a complete stranger, shaking his finger in front of Xiang Nan's nose and criticising him without mercy. Obviously, the draft address commissioned by the central leadership of the CYL and received with universal approval had now become Xiang Nan's 'anti-party materials'. In the same way, this article, which had gone to other central party leaders on the authority of the CYL's central leaders and had then been circulated throughout the ranks of the party, now became the responsibility of Xiang Nan and Xiang Nan alone.

For more than six months, the central leadership of the CYL conducted unceasing criticism of Xiang Nan, in meetings large and small. They hauled out all of Xiang Nan's reports and articles, written over many years, ruthlessly quoting them out of context, twisting his words into all sorts of 'anti-party' statements. Before announcing Xiang Nan's punishment, the CYL's leaders convened a criticism session at the league's party school, involving more than 2,000 people, to continue the denunciation of Xiang Nan. They went so far as to notify Wang Zhixin that she was expected to speak at the criticism session targeting her husband.

Wang Zhixin was herself an important cadre in the CYL's central administration. Demanding that she be present for this gigantic criticism session aimed at Xiang Nan, and that she publicly "draw a clear line between herself and Xiang Nan", as the phrase used at that time said, was unspeakably bitter for her. If she refused to criticise Xiang Nan and refused publicly to 'draw a line' between herself and her husband, she knew what would happen: she, too, would become a 'rightist element'. If the two of them were thus brought down, what would happen to their entire family, elders and children alike?

Just at this moment of the most extreme pain and conflict, Wang Zhixin suddenly received a notice from the CYL's central administrative office, ordering her to accompany Hu Yaobang, first secretary of the CYL, on an inspection mission to Xushui county in the province of Hebei. As soon as she received this message, like a drowning person clinging to a life ring, Wang Zhixin suddenly heaved a sigh of relief.

By the time Wang Zhixin returned from accompanying Hu Yaobang to Xushui, the criticism session had ended, and there was no point in her standing on the platform denouncing Xiang Nan. As she looked back on it later, that business trip had had absolutely nothing to do with her work; it was Hu Yaobang's way of helping Wang make her way through this most extreme of difficulties. Decades later, remembering those old events, Wang Zhixin's heart was still filled with gratitude.

Chapter 17

Sent Down to Labour in the Beijing Dongjiao State Farm

Labelled a 'rightist element', Xiang Nan was quickly dispatched to the Beijing Dongjiao (Eastern Suburbs) state farm to 'participate in labour'. In 1957, most of the 'rightist elements' were people from outside the party or intellectuals. By 1958, many leading cadres from the party itself were swept up. But of the true 'rightist element' high cadres in Beijing who held the rank of vice-minister or higher, only a few were 'sent down' to perform manual work on the farms.

Xiang Nan on the Beijing Dongjiao state farm, 1961

In his three years of farm labour, Xiang Nan formed deep friendships with the cadres, staff and workers on the farm. This photo shows Xiang Nan with the secretary of the farm's party committee, Li Zhongpu

Xiang Nan departed for farm labour in the Beijing Dongjiao state farm on the eve of China's national day holiday, 1 October 1958. Everyone was making ready to celebrate the holiday. Although Wang Zhixin's heart was heavy, she packed a few things for Xiang Nan and sent him off to report to the farm.

Wang Zhixin and Xiang Nan had walked the same path together ever since the war. They had experienced the Japanese and puppet armies' great 'cleanup campaigns', and had undergone the rectification campaign in northern Subei, the great political self-examination process that so many had undergone. No matter how difficult the external environment, and no matter how many wrongs they had suffered, Xiang Nan always comforted her optimistically, telling her: "Everything is going to turn out all right."

As a member of the CYL's central leadership, Wang Zhixin had herself participated in the third plenum of the league's third central committee, and had watched the unending criticism of her husband. As the investigations continued over and over, her heart suffered as though torn by a knife's blade. When a 'rightist elements' dunce cap was placed on Xiang Nan's head, it was as though her family was being drowned.

Xiang Nan with young farmer labourers on the commune

Although Wang Zhixin was frail in appearance, in her heart she was utterly strong. Xiang Nan, always so busy and active, suddenly had nothing to do. Usually such a vigorous talker, now he could find no one with whom he could talk.

At that time, Wang Zhixin's greatest fear was that Xiang Nan would not be able to cope with the extreme political pressure directed against him. What gave her consolation was that, aside from the seemingly endless burden of having to write his self-criticism, Xiang Nan was still able to read books and newspapers each day. He even set about putting in order a vast number of photographs that he had taken over the years, carefully placing each one into a photo album. But, in the cloistered courtyards of the central party leadership's compound, no one could hear the sound of Xiang Nan's hearty laughter.

Xiang Nan in 1961, during his stint as a farm labourer in the Beijing Dongjiao state farm, at the Agricultural Exhibition Hall with the deputy chief of the central committee propaganda department Zhang Panshi (third from right), the secretary of the Chaoyang district party committee Liu Yuman (second from right), and the head of Xiang Nan's farm Li Zhongpu (far right)

Xiang Nan with Li Zhongpu (left), head of the Beijing Dongjiao state farm, and another farm leader, 1961

Xiang Nan at work on a dam-building site during his years 'sent down' from his former posts

Every time he did return to the party leaders' courtyards, an ineradicable shadow haunted him. When he returned to the farm on the outskirts of Beijing, he became a different person. Looking upon his flourishing plot of land, the simple and honest farmers and workers of his farm, and those farm leaders who relied on and put their trust in him, Xiang Nan managed to recover his confidence and his self-respect. There on the farm, no one treated him as a 'rightist element' and no one dwelt upon the 'errors' he had been accused of committing.

At heart, Xiang Nan was a son of the mountains, and the child of peasants. He quickly built rapport with the farm labourers, and became one of the core figures among the farm's leaders. In the minds of those leaders, Zheng Cong and Li Zhongpu, even though Xiang Nan had not been assigned by higher authorities to serve as a leader of the farm, he was recognised as exactly that: a 'leader'. They discussed all farm questions great and small with him. On many questions, the farm's party committee admitted him to their discussions and made their decisions on the basis of his remarks. And so, everyone came affectionately to call Xiang Nan, 'Boss Xiang'.

The entire happy family in the 1960s. From right to left: Xiang Nan, Xiang Xiaoqing, Xiang Xiaolan, Wang Zhixin, Xiang Xiaolü, Xiang Xiaobai, Wang Cunyu (Xiang Nan's mother), Xiang Xiaomi and Xiang Xiaohong

The Dongjiao farm was one of the first state farms to be established. In 1958, the Laiguangying people's commune was merged into the Beijing Dongjiao state farm, and the combined unit took the name Peace people's commune. Subsequently, it was renamed the Sino-Albanian Friendship people's commune. Soon after Xiang Nan arrived there, the farm received a message: "Beware of the words and deeds of the 'rightist element' Xiang Nan." It did not take long for everyone to see that this was a good fellow; how could someone like this possibly be a bad man?

In the opinion of the leader of the farm, Zheng Cong, Xiang Nan's manner was devoid of affectation, and in fact he was sometimes mischievous; he simply did not resemble a high-ranking leader.

The farm had a motorcycle at that time. At first, Xiang Nan was able to return home once or twice a month, with Zheng Cong ferrying him to Beijing on the motorcycle. After a time, Xiang Nan learned to ride it himself, and now and then rode home on it. One time, on the airport road, he nearly had a disaster.

On that particular day, some foreign dignitary had arrived. The police had shut down the entire road to the airport. Who would have imagined that, on this very day, Xiang Nan would be driving onto the airport road from the side road that led to his farm? When the police spotted a motorcyclist wearing a windbreaker and sunglasses driving onto the closed highway, they got agitated, and set out in their police cars in hot pursuit. When Xiang Nan caught sight of the police cars coming his way, he knew things looked bad, so he sped off. Knowing the local geography intimately, he disappeared like a puff of smoke into the crops growing by the side of the highway, and made his way back to the farm on smaller roads. Later, when the police showed up to inquire, everyone claimed not to have seen the man in question.

In 1958, the Beijing Dongjiao state farm, with its favourable natural conditions and strong foundations in farming and animal husbandry, joined the Great Leap Forward by establishing a communal dining hall. Even old women with bound feet had to walk as much as a mile to the dining hall for each meal. After Xiang Nan saw this, he consulted with the farm's leaders, and the communal dining hall was eliminated.

Xiang Nan, his wife and their son Xiang Xiaolü climb the Great Wall, 1960s

Xiang Nan and Wang Zhixin at the Summer Palace in Beijing, 1957

The former head of the Beijing state farm administration bureau, Liu Ming, was then nominally assisting in running the Beijing Dongjiao state farm. He and Xiang Nan had become intimate friends, able to talk about anything and everything. In his memoirs, Liu Ming later wrote: "When Xiang Nan was sent down here, you could see nothing wrong with him. He spoke with his usual cheerfulness, and took a close interest in the nation's affairs. Actually in his second year, the Beijing state farm administration bureau assigned a deputy to serve him on the Beijing Dongjiao state farm, but he continued to carry out the 'three togethers' [eating together, living together, working together] with the farm labourers. Xiang Nan had the habit of reading great quantities of news in the papers every day. He browsed all the papers that the farm subscribed to, in one sitting. Generally, he returned to Beijing once a month, and in his off hours he would sit in his tiny room and read books and newspapers."

After the Beijing Dongjiao state farm became the Sino-Albanian friendship commune, it was not unusual for foreign guests to visit. The farm's leaders often allowed Xiang Nan to accompany the visitors. Xiang had travelled abroad, and had often been involved in foreign activities as a member of the CYL's central leadership, so he could converse easily with foreigners. On one occasion, this led a foreign guest to observe with amazement: "China is really marvellous. Even the leaders of state farms have such high qualifications!"

During the Great Leap Forward, the shrieking gales of exaggeration caused some people to abandon caution. For his part, Xiang Nan kept his feet firmly planted on the ground. He urged people not to listen to false propaganda, and encouraged them to do their farm work well, in accordance with the laws of production. At that time, the highest authorities called for farmers to adopt 'deep ploughing'. Newspaper editorials claimed that this farming technique would greatly increase crop yields. Xiang Nan did not believe a word of it. He said that deep-ploughed soil would be raw; how could crops be planted in it? Everyone discussed this, and agreed to pay only lip service to the investigations by higher authorities, without actually deep-ploughing the soil. As a result, the following year, the farms and communes that had deep-ploughed suffered severely reduced yields over large areas. Only on the Beijing Dongjiao state farm had deep ploughing been avoided; by contrast, harvests were very good. Everyone admired Xiang Nan for his foresight.

Xiang Nan and Wang Zhixin in Beijing, 1960s

By 1960, the terrible results of the Great Leap Forward were clear. The entire nation fell into a great famine. To lighten Wang Zhixin's burdens, Xiang Nan brought his eldest son Xiang Xiaohong to a middle school near his farm. There was not enough grain to eat. But some of the farm's agricultural workers managed to send peanuts, sweet potatoes, eggs and the like to Xiang Nan and his son. This gave Xiang Nan's household a few food items that, for urban dwellers, in the midst of the food shortages engulfing the entire country, were precious treasures. In the memories of Xiang Nan's children, the Beijing Dongjiao state farm had thus been a paradise. During the holidays, when they went to see their father, he taught them how to drive tractors and horse carts, and went on expeditions with them to hunt for strawberries. Their father never complained about anything to them; the smallest of the children never knew why their father had gone to the farm, and thought that for Xiang Nan it was just a matter of changing jobs.

A photo taken by Xiang Nan of his family, including his mother, Wang Cunyu, (back row, second from left), his wife and their six children. On the far right is Wang Zhixin's father, the children's maternal grandfather

Chapter 18

The Courage and Insight of Minister Chen Zhengren

Chen Zhengren, minister of the eighth ministry of machine building, in front of the entrance to his residence at 10 Wanshou Road, 1962

Xiang Nan left the Beijing Dongjiao state farm at the end of 1961.

One day early in the winter, Xiang Nan received a phone call from organisation bureau of the party centre, asking him to go to the eighth ministry of machine building (that is the agricultural machinery industry ministry) and report to Minister Chen Zhengren. Xiang Nan rushed to find Zheng Cong and asked Zheng to take him to the ministry on his motorcycle.

Xiang Nan and Chen Zhengren talked for two hours before Xiang emerged. As soon as he saw Xiang Nan's beaming face, Zheng Cong knew something good had happened. Before Zheng could open his mouth, Xiang Nan said: "Let's go to a restaurant!" In those years, eating in a restaurant was a real extravagance. The years of hardship were not yet over. The blotchy complexions of the people in the streets were a sign of their inadequate nutrition. After so many years of close acquaintance, this was the first time that the frugal Xiang Nan had ever invited Zheng Cong to a restaurant for a meal.

The two men sat down, and Xiang Nan said to Zheng Cong: "The organisation has arranged a new job for me, in the general office of the eighth ministry of machine building. Minister Chen and I talked at length. Did you know about it? Minister Chen is an imposing figure. He's got great credentials. He is an old revolutionary from the early days in the Jinggang mountains, and was chairman of the Jiangxi soviet."

One can only admire Cheng Zhengren's courage in arranging for such a famous 'rightist element' as Xiang Nan to leave his farm and move to the eighth ministry, and then to appoint Xiang deputy director of the ministry's general office as soon as he arrived. Those who had known him from earlier times understood that doing this took great political courage. In those days, people were terrified of the 'rightist element' label. Would any other minister have had the courage to bring a 'rightist element' to work at his side?

It was Hu Yaobang who recommended Xiang Nan to Chen Zhengren.

Labelling Xiang Nan and Liang Buting as 'rightist elements' had left Hu Yaobang deeply unsettled. These two men were the cadres closest to him. They were mainly responsible for writing the major documents of the CYL's central leadership. Liang Buting had made a soft landing, and his punishments were later cancelled; he remained in the league's central organisation. But Xiang Nan's case was different. Originally, he was stripped of his posts and sent down to the Beijing Dongjiao state farm. After the Lushan plenum of the party's central committee in 1959, on orders from higher authority in the party, the penalties for Xiang Nan as a 'rightist element' were increased. He was demoted two ranks in the party's administrative structure. That meant a reduction of his wages by several tens of yuan. Xiang Nan had a big family, and his burdens were heavy; this demotion simply added insult to injury

When the campaign of criticism of the 'Ten Opinions' was underway, Xiang Nan took full responsibility, in reality assuming the responsibility that rightfully belonged to the CYL's central secretariat. Long afterwards, Hu Yaobang put his energies to work to try to rehabilitate Xiang Nan. But Hu's strenuous efforts vanished like a burst bubble, as the 10th plenum of the eighth CPC central committee re-ignited the 'class struggle' theme and furious criticism of Peng Dehuai erupted over Peng's 80,000-word appeal for the reversal of the party's verdicts against him.

Hu Yaobang still managed to find an opportunity. On 19 July 1961, the party centre issued a *Critical Report on Some Policy Questions Arising in Natural Science Work*, calling for re-examination of the cases of intellectuals who had been wrongly criticised in the preceding several years. Following these instructions, when word emerged that a national work conference on the reforming of 'rightist elements' was being called by the party's united front, organisation and publicity departments, Hu Yaobang decided that the time was right for resolving the question of Xiang Nan's work.

Xiang Nan and Minister Chen Zhengren of the eighth ministry of machine building at 10 Wanshou Road in Beijing, 1962

Hu Yaobang knew that it would be impossible to bring Xiang Nan back to the CYL's central body, and Xiang Nan himself was unwilling to return to work there. But what ministry or commission would have Xiang Nan? Hu Yaobang thought of Chen Zhengren at the eighth ministry. This was an old-time leading cadre who 'sought truth from facts' and protected the cadres under him. Chen Zhengren had been part of the creation of the revolutionary base area in the Jinggang mountains. Even Mao Zedong had warmly referred to him as an "old wartime comrade in arms".

At a meeting, Hu Yaobang sought out Chen Zhengren and told him of Xiang Nan's situation. Chen responded at once: "Let's make Xiang Nan the head of the college of agricultural machinery."

Hu shook his head. He told Chen: "It would be a shame to send Xiang Nan to the agricultural machinery college. He is a rare talent and a great writer. It would be better if you placed him at your side."

Chen Zhengren closed the matter: "Fine. We'll make him deputy director of the ministry's administrative office."

And in that way, Xiang Nan left the Beijing Dongjiao state farm, ended more than three years of 'sent down' manual work, and reported for duty at the eighth ministry of machine building.

Chapter 19

Compiling a Series of Research Reports on Agricultural Mechanisation

The eighth ministry of machine building was originally called the ministry of agricultural machinery industry. It was set up in 1959. The list of government units under the jurisdiction of the state council did not originally include a ministry for agricultural machinery. But on 4 April 1959, Mao Zedong put out a letter, in the form of an 'internal party bulletin', to the entire party organisation, from the provincial level down through the regions, counties, communes, big production brigades and even the small local production brigades. In the letter, Mao raised the idea that "fundamentally, the salvation of agriculture lies in mechanisation". He went on: "Looking at the decade ahead, we must achieve small solutions in four years, solve medium-sized challenges within seven years and achieve big solutions in less than 10 years."

In August 1959, in its decision establishing plans for the national economy, the eighth plenum of the eighth central committee established a set of relative priorities for dealing with various issues in agricultural development. Again, Chairman Mao raised the matter of creating a ministry of agricultural machine building. Mao finally went so far as to claim that, if no one could be found to serve as minister, he would take the job himself.

Chen Zhengren, who was then serving as deputy director of the party's rural work department, asked to be assigned the task of organising the new ministry. In 1965, the ministry's name was formally changed to the eighth ministry of machine building.

During his years working in the central organisation of the CYL, Xiang Nan had joined Hu Yaobang on several inspection visits to large-scale state-owned industrial enterprises such as the First Auto Works in Changchun, Anshan Iron and Steel, the Fulaerji Heavy Machinery plant in Qiqihar, the Luoyang Tractor works, the Luoyang Mining Equipment factory, the Karamay oil field and the Lanzhou oil refinery. He felt deep pride at the industrial accomplishments of the new China. More than once, he had entertained the idea of throwing himself heart and soul into the industrial development of the motherland.

Xiang Nan (fourth from left) with Chen Zhengren (third from right) and Chen's wife Peng Ru (fifth from right) and the children of these close comrades, at Beidaihe in 1962

Once he reached the eighth ministry, Xiang Nan was as full of idealism and enthusiasm, and as modest, as a primary school student. He studied hard and bored deeply into the question of agricultural mechanisation. In pursuit of his tasks, he made the acquaintance of many agricultural machinery experts and sought their advice. Originally a novice, he soon developed real competence in his field.

Chen Zhengren was a deeply experienced leader, with a solid, steady work style and a talent for investigation and research. He spent about four months of every year doing his own fact-finding at the grassroots level. As soon as he arrived at the eighth ministry, Xiang Nan began accompanying the minister on his grassroots inspection trips. Familiar as he had become with China's agricultural machinery situation, and given his grasp of a great deal of firsthand material, Xiang Nan quickly became Chen Zhengren's competent assistant.

After a year on the job, with Chen Zhengren's encouragement, Xiang published a dense article in September 1962 entitled 'Scientific Research Work on Agricultural Mechanisation Must Pave the Way for Mechanisation'. The article was widely praised. From that point on, Xiang Nan began his assiduous and deep explorations of the policy issues surrounding agricultural mechanisation.

Some months later, he published an even weightier article in *People's Daily* under the title 'Some Questions Regarding Agricultural Mechanisation'. This article examined in detail, under 12 headings, the problems that China was facing in developing agricultural mechanisation, and the policies needed to deal with them, including 'agricultural collectivisation and agricultural mechanisation', 'pathways and methods', 'needs and measures', 'economic resources and technology policies', and 'scientific research and technological personnel'.

In his article, Xiang Nan wrote: "We must pay attention to the introduction of agricultural machinery products from other countries, collect the most up-to-date scientific information and utilise the useful experiences of all countries." In the latter section of this long article, Xiang Nan drew a blueprint for China's realisation of agricultural mechanisation.

Xiang Nan was adept at operating all kinds of agricultural machines. The photo shows him driving a Chinese-made tractor while performing manual work

"Agricultural mechanisation requires a new kind of human being, not only able to master modern technologies, but possessed of a new kind of moral nature deeply infused with the spirit of collectivism. How many of these new people do we need? If we start with conceptual design, scientific research, manufacturing, practical management, then move on to the essential support functions of supply and distribution, transportation and capital construction, and finally add all the related training schools, we can get an idea of how many scientists, engineers, technical personnel, manufacturing workers, tractor drivers, managers and educators we will need. These numbers could reach several million. We can say that agricultural mechanisation aims to transform China's hundreds of millions of rural dwellers into cultured workers equipped with socialist consciousness. They will form the greatest modernised agricultural army in the world. This will be a far-reaching revolution, made possible by technological revolution."

Mao Zedong was very much concerned with agricultural mechanisation. This article caught his attention, and also left a very deep impression on a number of party leaders equally concerned with the problems of agriculture and agricultural mechanisation. Several years later, Hu Yaobang brought up the article in a conversation with Xiang Nan.

After a year at the eighth ministry, Chen Zhengren, who had an eye for talent, appointed Xiang Nan to be the head of the bureau of agricultural mechanisation within the ministry, with direct responsibility for production and management in the agricultural machinery sector.

In his four years at the eighth ministry, Xiang Nan poured his energies into his work. Every year, he and the leadership team in the ministry spent a third of their time together at the grassroots level, assiduously examining the advancement of the nation's agricultural mechanisation and the laws of science, adherence to which was essential for continued progress.

From November 1963 to March 1964, Xiang Nan spent five months visiting villages and rural enterprises in Henan, Hubei, Hunan, Guangdong and Guangxi. Then he moved on to Inner Mongolia, Liaoning, Jilin and Heilongjiang to examine agricultural machinery production and utilisation. He wrote a series of articles for *People's Daily* and the magazine *China's Agricultural Mechanisation*, entitled 'On Stable Yields, High Yields and Agricultural Mechanisation', 'A Re-examination of Stable Yields, High

Yields and Agricultural Mechanisation' and 'A Research Report on the Problems of Agricultural Mechanisation'. These essays provided useful guidance on the development of the agricultural machinery sector.

Xiang Nan maintained unwavering clarity on the central issues: how to build agricultural mechanisation on very backward foundations, and how to grope forward towards a path to agricultural mechanisation that was suitable to China's national conditions.

In September 1962, he wrote an investigation report, 'Things We Have Learned About Farm Wheelbarrows'. In rural villages in those days, a tiny wheelbarrow could solve very big production problems.

According to Xiang Nan's investigations, roughly 40% of all village labour was spent in transportation. But in many broad areas, the people still relied on wheelbarrows with wooden wheels, much as they had done for 2,000 years. Even when small-capacity carts with rubber tyres were available, because of a lack of understanding of the peasants' customs, they did not sell well. For reasons like this, Xiang Nan's report took up four themes: 'Agricultural urgently needs transportation tools', 'The peasants like wheelbarrows with rubber wheels', 'What kind of rubber-wheeled wheelbarrows do the peasants like?' and 'Peasant opinions of rubber-wheeled barrows'. He laid out his view that every segment of the production and distribution of rubber-wheeled wheelbarrows had to be improved. His article was warmly received both by the factories that produced such equipment and by the masses of farmers themselves.

Chen Zhengren and Xiang Nan were the pioneers in the field of agricultural mechanism during that era. The great agricultural mechanisation project that they led thus took its first steps with such tiny rubber-tyred wheelbarrows.

Chapter 20

A Year on the Ground at the Luoyang Tractor Factory

In 1964, Xiang Nan and Chen Zhengren went to be 'on the ground' at the Luoyang First Tractor factory, as participants in the 'socialist education movement'. This period 'on the ground', which lasted nearly a year, was not the usual kind of research mission. Instead, it was a genuine way of entering fully into the work of the masses. They respectfully took the workers and the factory's technical personnel as their teachers, combined labour with technical learning and learned management skills.

Xiang Nan (back row, fourth from left) and Chen Zhengren (front, third from left) at the Luoyang Tractor factory during their 'on the ground' sojourn, 1964

A Year on the Ground at the Luoyang Tractor Factory

Xiang Nan and Minister Chen Zhengren moved the eighth ministry's administrative office to Luoyang. They lived in simple visitors' quarters at the plant, ate three meals a day with the workers in the factory dining hall, went to work and came off their shifts with the workers. Because they accepted no special treatment, the workers at the Luoyang Tractor factory formed high opinions of them.

On 4 December 1964, Chen Zhengren wrote a report to the party central authorities, recounting the knowledge gained during the months 'on the ground'. On 29 January 1965, Mao Zedong signified his approval of what Chen Zhengren had done in penetrating deeply into the productive lives of the masses of the workers. He appended several instructions of his own to Chen's report. He wrote: "If managerial personnel do not go into the small working groups on the factory floor to realise the 'Three Togethers', learning one or more special skills from the workers who are their teachers, they will remain forever locked in bitter struggle with the working class, and they will ultimately be labelled capitalists and the workers will overthrow them. If they don't learn technology, they will remain outsiders for a long time. It is not acceptable for them to handle their managerial tasks badly, trying to manage others while they themselves remain ignorant."

The year 'on the ground' enabled Xiang Nan to advance his understanding of production management issues in a large-scale manufacturer of equipment. On 4 January 1965, the first plenum of the third NPC passed a resolution, changing the name of the ministry of agricultural machinery industry to the eighth ministry of machine building. No matter what name changes took place, to Xiang Nan, the future of agricultural mechanisation was bright and full of hope.

Chapter 21

The 'Xinzhou Experience' and the Ideals of Agricultural Mechanisation

After the founding of the new China, Mao Zedong and the CPC members of his generation pondered deeply the question of how to feed and clothe hundreds of millions of people in the world's most populous nation.

In May 1950, in order to restore agricultural production as quickly as possible after the devastation left by years of war, the party centre and the government administrative council of the central people's government conducted a 50-day exhibition of modern agricultural implements in the Zhongnanhai leadership compound. Leaders from the party, the government and the military all attended.

Two men were pictured on the cover of the August 1950 edition of the magazine *China Pictorial*. One was the female tractor driver Liang Jun, who later became famous. The image of Liang boldly driving her tractor into the fields was printed in calendars and new year's celebratory posters; she became a symbol of her era. All of these developments are evidence of the emphasis that the new nation's leaders placed on improving agricultural equipment and gradually advancing agricultural mechanisation.

Xiang Nan was influenced as a child by the educational thinking of Tao Xingzhi, and driven in his youth by the ideal of repaying his debt to the motherland by building up commercial enterprises. Once he joined the revolution, Xiang Nan embraced unquestioningly Lenin's views on 'electrification of the soviets'. Twice, on returning from visits to the USSR, Xiang glowingly described to young Chinese audiences the Soviet Union's industrial development and the mechanisation of its collective agriculture. He encouraged his young listeners to throw themselves wholeheartedly into the great task of rural development.

The 'Xinzhou Experience' and the Ideals of Agricultural Mechanisation

In 1955, the young translator Cao Ying translated the novel by the Soviet writer Galina Nikolayeva, *The Head of the Machine Tractor Station and the Female Chief Agronomist*, into Chinese. With the support of Hu Yaobang and Xiang Nan, the novel was published serially in the magazine *China Youth*, which had a 3m circulation. Subsequently, the China Youth Publishing House printed the entire novel, with a first print run of 1,240,000. That broke the standing record for printings of translated novels. Nastasia, the heroine of the novel, became a role model for the young people of that era.

Over his five years at the eighth ministry, Xiang Nan carried out deep investigations in many provinces and regions nationwide. He read vast amounts of material on theories of agricultural mechanisation and on agricultural mechanisation in other countries. With Chen Zhengren's encouragement, he carried out active explorations of the ways in which the agricultural machinery sector in China should proceed.

While visiting Hubei province in 1963, he learned from the province's leaders that the county of Xinzhou had achieved impressive increases in cotton production thanks to agricultural mechanisation. So he decided to make a special trip to Xinzhou, where he spent some time investigating and studying. He discovered a model of agricultural mechanisation at the Xinzhou Liuji commune that became known as the 'Xinzhou experience'. He himself wrote an essay summing up what he had learned at Xinzhou, and published it in *People's Daily*.

In his analysis of Xinzhou's agricultural mechanisation, Xiang Nan identified two principal experiences. The first was that Xinzhou had carefully pondered the problem of how to proceed with agricultural mechanisation in a place where population was high and land was scarce. Putting it in concrete terms, they had come up with a strategy that mixed mechanisation and semi-mechanisation, with labour as the main given. They started by working on irrigation and drainage; employed 'comprehensive utilisation' techniques to maximise the utility of all production inputs; developed agricultural side production and processing; brought mechanisation to threshing and crop protection; and at one and the same time pursued improved cultivation techniques and the mechanisation of transport functions. This is a big difference from those places where population is sparse and land plentiful, which start their agricultural mechanisation with crop cultivation and transportation.

The second experience that Xiang Nan derived from his observations in Xinzhou was that agricultural mechanisation there had not depended on the state; what was done was done mainly through self-reliance, using the economic power of the collective, and fully drawing on the untapped strengths of the people's commune and its constituent production brigades.

Xiang Nan's summing up of the 'Xinzhou experience' turned Xinzhou into a national model as universally known as the Dazhai Production Brigade.[1] Xiang Nan's article provided a major stimulus to the leaders of Hubei province in pursuing the mechanisation of agriculture. They began to apply the 'Xinzhou experience' more broadly, and the Liuji commune became a symbolic red banner for the entire nation's agricultural mechanisation.

On 5 February 1966, the Hubei provincial party committee reported to the party centre on its step-by-step achievement of its plan for agricultural mechanisation. The report gained Mao Zedong's close attention and, after reading the document, Mao wrote the following instruction:

> *Comrade Wang Renzhong,*
> *I have read this item and think it is very good. Please send it to comrade [Liu] Shaoqi and ask him to decide whether it should be distributed to party committees in all provinces, cities and regions for study. All provinces, municipalities and regions should formulate five-year, seven-year and 10-year plans for accomplishing agricultural mechanisation fundamentally through self-reliance. A few pilot projects should be established and then expanded, so that agricultural mechanisation can be fundamentally achieved within 25 years. After 25 years, there will be no boundaries and by that time our essential orienting ideas are likely to be very different. Most probably, the theme will be 'The time has come for a new 25-year plan, resting on the foundations of what has been accomplished over the past 25 years.' Right now, we are looking at 15 years of intense work ahead of us. Ten years have already passed. We have not done very well over the past decade.*
>
> *Mao Zedong*
> *19 February 1966*

The 'Xinzhou Experience' and the Ideals of Agricultural Mechanisation

According to Mao Zedong's schedule, China was to have accomplished basic agricultural mechanisation by 1980.

To move ahead on Mao's instruction, the eighth ministry convened a conference on planning the management of the nation's agricultural mechanisation. The meeting debated the document known as *Main Points in the Third Five-year Plan Outline for Agricultural Mechanisation*. At the meeting, Xiang Nan's presentation, 'Use Mao Zedong Thought as a Guide, Reach Beyond the Limitations of Other Countries' Experiences, and Follow Our Own Path' discussed in comprehensive terms a vision of how agricultural modernisation ought to be realised.

In his report, Xiang Nan pointed out: "With respect to how we go about achieving agricultural mechanisation, Chairman Mao has written about this in a comprehensive and systematic way. We have recently gathered together as many as 40 of his writings that deal directly or indirectly with these questions."

In the spirit of Mao Zedong's speech and his instructions, Xiang Nan carefully, methodically and boldly put forth in his address to the conference his scheme for accelerating and raising the overall level of agricultural mechanisation:

"If we think of this in terms of all our provinces and regions, in the coming five years we will have energetically grasped the challenge of developing the agricultural machinery sector. We will have achieved basic agricultural mechanisation in the Pearl and Yangtze river delta areas and in greater Beijing and greater Shanghai. Within seven years, the provinces of Hubei, Guangdong and Jiangsu, as well as the three provinces of the northeast and Xinjiang, will have achieved agricultural mechanisation. By the 10th year, the vast majority of our provinces and autonomous regions will have gained basic agricultural mechanisation. Some provinces and regions may take 15 years to achieve that."

At that time, Xiang Nan and all other highly ranked party cadres took Mao Zedong's target date of 1980 for the full realisation of agricultural mechanisation without any qualms. From the perspective of that time, it was not some sort of far-fetched, empty utopian idea. It was based on the solid foundation of the development of the farm machinery sector over the preceding decade.

Between 1966 and 1978, the party centre and the state council convened three national conferences on agricultural mechanisation. Xiang Nan attended all three and was one of the drafters of the major documents produced at each conference.

If it had not been for the 10 years of chaos and the wholesale economic retreat they caused, which put the agricultural mechanisation targets beyond reach, great strides toward these goals would have been achieved. Sadly, the perpetual political ferment of the 1960s and 1970s, and the near collapse of the economy, made achievement of those goals increasingly uncertain.

Chapter 22

The Nightmare Years of the 'Cultural Revolution'

Once the 'Cultural Revolution' had erupted, Xiang Nan, Chen Zhengren and a large group of cadres were labelled as part of the 'faction of powerholders taking the capitalist road'. They became the targets of severe criticism by 'rebel' factions in the eighth ministry.

During the 'Cultural Revolution', Xiang Nan was labelled a 'powerholder taking the capitalist road'. In 1969, he laboured at the May 7 cadre school in Yilan county, Heilongjiang province

Xiang Nan had already borne the 'rightist element' dunce cap, making it even harder for him to escape from the 'Cultural Revolution'.

In 1967, Xiang Nan was placed in the cowshed, a term used exclusively in the 'Cultural Revolution' to refer to a prison set up by rebels for various 'bad characters'. However, that was not the end of his struggles. Not only did he undergo ceaseless criticism sessions, but he had to perform heavy labour under the watchful eye of the 'rebel' faction. Approaching the age of 50, he carried loads of more than 100kg from trucks and carts. On one occasion, Xiang Nan tumbled into a hole while bearing a huge load, and he was unable to climb out for half a day. Xiang Nan had long suffered from an inflammation of a heart membrane, and amid the chaos he suffered terribly. He aged very rapidly.

Wang Zhixin allowed her children to visit Xiang Nan and send him things to eat. But the rebels drove them away time after time. Over two full years, except for the one time when their second daughter Xiang Xiaomi was lucky enough to see her father, no one in his family ever laid eyes on him. Xiang Nan's salary was cut back and the family's savings were frozen. Nine people in their household depended entirely on the income of one person – Wang Zhixin. The financial hardships of their lives can easily be imagined.

Xiang Nan working at the Xinyang May 7 cadre school in Henan

In the face of the national catastrophe that was the 'Cultural Revolution', Wang Zhixin displayed rare calm. In 1969, she was about to be sent away for manual work at the state council's May 7 cadre school at Pingluo in the remote Ningxia Hui autonomous region. She and Xiang Nan discussed what arrangements to make for the children. Their oldest daughter Xiang Xiaoqing went with her father to Yilan, while their son Xiang Xiaobai and their second daughter Xiang Xiaom went with their mother to Ningxia. Their youngest child Xiang Xiaolü remained in Beijing with his grandmother to go to school. Yet, in these years of disorder, Xiang Nan and Wang Zhixin still taught their children to have faith in the future of their nation and its people, encouraging them to study even more and not to waste their opportunities to learn.

At the May 7 cadre school in Xinyang, Henan province, no one was able to drive the tractors in the tractor station. Xiang Nan volunteered to drive them; his skills could be put to use. In those days, tractors were not only used for ploughing the fields; they were used even more for transportation and hauling.

Xiang Nan at first drove the tractors as transporters on paved roads, while senior cadres working in the fields watched with envy. One time, when Xiang Nan was driving along the border of Huangchuan county, he caught sight of a familiar figure from behind. Could it be Hu Yaobang? At that very moment, Hu was struggling to haul a heavy cart onto the roadway.

Xiang Nan hastily pulled to a stop by the roadside and stepped forward, calling to Hu Yaobang. The two men had not met in years, and never dreamed they would run into each other in a situation like this. They were overcome with emotion and for a while stood

Xiang Nan at home in Beijing, after his release in 1970 and his return to agricultural mechanisation work

speechless. Finally, Hu Yaobang broke the silence. He said to Xiang Nan with a smile: "You're still the same person. You can drive a tractor. That's mechanisation. People like me can only transport things with shoulder poles."

Seeing that they were alone, the two men sat down on the road to talk. They said almost nothing about their personal affairs. What gripped them was the future and the destiny of the nation.

Not long after, Xiang Nan's own destiny finally met with an unexpected opportunity. One day in late 1970, a military representative suddenly ordered him back to Beijing, stating that a new position had been arranged for him. As it turned out, Mao Zedong had not forgotten his preoccupation with agricultural mechanisation even amid the disorder of the 'Cultural Revolution'. Under such circumstances, it was ultimately necessary to put a leader with specialised knowledge in charge of carrying out the task of agricultural mechanisation.

As soon as he got back to Beijing, various people came to talk with Xiang Nan about how to arrange a position for him. The first thing he

Xiang Nan, his wife and mother and his children in Beijing, 1970s

heard about was a job as deputy general director of construction on the Baoji-Chengdu railway project. Xiang Nan knew nothing about railway construction, but the party organisation left him no choice but to obey. Just as he was packing a few items and preparing to go to his assignment, things changed once again. He was kept in Beijing and retained on the agricultural mechanisation task, with an appointment as the head of a 'leading small group' within the first ministry of machine building.

Long before the 'Cultural Revolution', Xiang Nan had crossed paths with Hua Guofeng, who was then in the party secretariat of Hunan province in charge of agriculture. Xiang Nan's abilities and his knowledge in the area of agricultural mechanisation had made an impression on Hua Guofeng. In 1970, Hua became deputy head of the vital state council operations group, assisting Zhou Enlai in managing the agricultural sector. While reviewing a list of senior cadres from revolutionary days, Hua had come across Xiang Nan's name. Looking at the list of Xiang Nan's postings, Hua decided that sending him out to handle railway matters was not appropriate. In reporting to Zhou Enlai on his work, Hua raised the idea of bringing Xiang Nan back to fill the agricultural mechanisation opening, and Zhou Enlai quickly concurred.

Xiang Nan at Loushanguan in Guizhou while on a work inspection visit, 1975

The ceaseless chaos had brought varying levels of destruction to the agricultural mechanisation process in various places across the country. Some factories, from the beginning of the 'Cultural Revolution', descended into ceaseless armed conflict and factional struggles; any kind of effective production management system was denounced as dogmatic and dictatorial. Under circumstances like these, Xiang Nan had lingering doubts, and made progress only with great difficulty.

Soon after, a Japanese delegation in the field of agricultural mechanisation visited China and asked to meet with

Xiang Nan visits the Longmen stone carvings in Luoyang during an inspection visit in 1975

Xiang Nan. They had read Xiang's articles on agricultural mechanisation and were very interested in his views. They hoped for a chance to meet him and exchange opinions. Within the first ministry of machine building, however, a vice-minister with strong 'leftist' credentials refused to allow Xiang Nan to meet with the visitors. He said: "This man Xiang Nan has a long history as a 'rightist'. How can we let him meet foreigners?" The vice-minister arranged for a deputy director in the general office who knew nothing about business to meet the foreign visitors. This deputy director had no choice but to seek out Xiang Nan for a basic introduction to the relevant issues, which he then shared with the Japanese.

This incident left Xiang Nan gloomy and depressed. He longed especially for Wang Zhixin, labouring in the remote May 7 cadre school in Pingluo, Ningxia, and his children. He asked his ministry for some time off and headed for Ningxia to see Wang Zhixin and the children.

It was already night-time when his train reached Yinchuan, the capital city of Ningxia. Xiang Nan found a small hotel for the night and early the next morning continued by train toward Pingluo. After many twists and turns, he finally found Wang Zhixin's military company.

Suddenly seeing Xiang Nan, Wang Zhixin could not believe her eyes. This couple, who had been through so much together, were overwhelmed by their feelings, magnified now by this precious moment of reunion. Each had a vast store of words to say. In the crude conditions of the May 7 cadre school, under the cold gaze of the military men in charge of Wang and the other workers, how could they find a place to be alone? Finally, near the May 7 school building, they spotted some large concrete pipes waiting to be installed as part of a water control engineering project. Xiang Nan had an idea. He and Wang Zhixin moved her bedding inside one of the concrete pipes, using a sheet as a curtain, and so created a temporary living space, a place where the two of them at least could have a chance to talk.

Chapter 23

A Path-breaker in the Liberation of Thinking

Before the policies of reform and opening up were introduced, Xiang Nan was one of only a few cadres of his rank at provincial or ministerial level to have opportunities to travel abroad.

In the 1950s, Xiang Nan visited the Soviet Union twice, and gained deep impressions of the country's heavy industry, collectivised agriculture and agricultural mechanisation. In 1957, he led a youth delegation to Japan, and saw with his own eyes the rapid development of its postwar economy.

Xiang Nan and his team visit the White Horse temple in Luoyang during a supervisory visit to Henan province. Far left is Xiang Nan's secretary, Lu Enqi

A Path-breaker in the Liberation of Thinking

Xiang Nan in San Francisco, 1976

On his return home, he told the leaders of the CYL what he had seen on his Japan visit, and how highly he regarded the Japanese economy. It was for these remarks that he was denounced as a 'rightist element' in 1958.

Plunged into years of adversity, Xiang Nan learned to think independently. What helped him most in this regard was his ability, in order to perform his work in the eighth ministry, to gain access to massive amounts of information on industrial developments all over the world. In those years of China's isolation, Xiang Nan's growing understanding of global technological developments was never interrupted.

Following the successful visit of US President Richard Nixon to China in 1972, China and the US opened the gates to a flow of mutual visits. In 1976, at the invitation of the Committee on Scholarly Exchange with the PRC, Xiang Nan travelled to the US as head of a study mission on American agriculture.

For this study mission, Xiang Nan made meticulous preparations. He specially asked an agriculture film studio to send a cinematographer and a film crew.

The go-betweens who made this visit possible were Joan Hinton and her husband Erwin Engst, who were then working in the agricultural mechanisation institute within the eighth ministry of machine building. The two had come to China before 1949 and had long worked on agricultural technology. They were good friends of Xiang Nan.

In 1948, Joan Hinton and her elder brother William, acting as land reform observers, had participated in the land reform movement in Lucheng county in Shanxi province. Their account at the time became a highly influential book in the West, entitled *Fanshen*. Because of their close affinities with red China, they suffered severely under McCarthyism when they returned to the US, and fell into financial difficulties. William Hinton ultimately returned to his home state of Pennsylvania, living as a farmer on his mother's farm.

After the Nixon visit to China, William Hinton visited China several times at the invitation of Zhou Enlai. Xiang Nan attended receptions in Hinton's honour, listening to Hinton's descriptions of his own farm. But without seeing it for himself, Xiang Nan could not imagine that a single man was able to cultivate 1,600 acres.

Xiang Nan during his visit to the US as leader of an agricultural mechanisation delegation

Seeing the doubts on the faces of the visiting Chinese delegation, Hinton joked: "So you are not accustomed to this? How many people would be needed to work a farm like mine in China? You would need to build a dining hall, a kindergarten, maybe a school. You would have to have a farm leader, and a chairman of the workers' association. Here, the farm leader is William Hinton. The engineer is William Hinton. The tractor driver is William Hinton. The truck driver is William Hinton. The accountant is William Hinton, too…"

Hinton's words drew a big laugh.

Hinton let the delegation's members have a look at his equipment: two heavy tractors, a planting machine, a harvester, a truck and irrigation equipment. He said that, during spring planting, he simply had to manage the sowing; everything else was up to the seed company. If the seeds did not sprout at the proper rate, the seed company had to pay compensation.

"What about weeding?" the delegation asked with concern, as they cast their eyes on a cornfield stretching to the horizon.

"We have a weed control company," Hinton replied. "As soon as the weeds appear, the company sends its airplane over to spray weed-killer. One year, they were careless and spread weed killer on our sunflower fields, killing a lot of our plants. They paid compensation."

Hinton explained that, after he had planted in the spring, he did not have much else to do. So he took to writing, working with the US-China People's Friendship Association on some projects, including visits to China, just to make use of his time. During autumn harvesting, sometimes he had his wife and children help out, but the children insisted on getting paid for the work...

Xiang Nan (front, far left) with his arm around William Hinton on Hinton's Pennsylvania farm during his visit to the US

Xiang Nan with William Hinton in Beijing, 1978

On his visit to the US in 1976, Xiang Nan not only led his team to study American farms, farm equipment manufacturing companies and agricultural research centres, but also visited the renowned American farm machinery company John Deere, and the Ford Motor Company in Detroit. He held introductory meetings with the National Council for US-China Trade (later known as the US-China Business Council) and officials at the US Department of Agriculture. What he saw and heard left him very stimulated. He could not but ponder this question: why was it that, in the capitalist US, science, technology and the economy had developed so rapidly, while the socialist PRC had remained so poor and backward for such a long time? How could America feed itself and produce such gigantic agricultural exports when farmers accounted for only 5% of its population?

In his trip diary, Xiang Nan wrote: "No matter how many people don't like the US or speak ill of the US, it is still the richest and most self-sufficient nation. Although it has experienced a quarter-century of struggle since liberation, China is still one of the world's poorest countries. Surpassing the US is still going to require enormous efforts for an extremely long time."

A Path-breaker in the Liberation of Thinking

Wrapping up their month-long visit to the US, Xiang Nan and his group returned home on 3 October 1976.

With the disorders of the 'Cultural Revolution' not yet over, and the sounds of the 'October thunderclap' not yet audible, Xiang Nan was already beginning to awaken to the enormous differences between the capitalist US and the socialist China. He felt an obligation to report all that he had seen, as well as his own thinking on the development of agricultural modernisation, in a frank report to the party centre and the leadership of the state council.

A few days later, the entire nation was immersed in rejoicing at the smashing of the 'Gang of Four', and the intense movement to denounce them quickly followed.

Xiang Nan's *Report on an Investigation of Agricultural Mechanisation in the US* was not transmitted by the first ministry of machine building and the ministry of agriculture and forestry to the relevant figures at the party centre until early the following year. Hua Guofeng, who was then the

Xiang Nan and his agricultural mechanisation delegation visit the famous US farm equipment manufacturer John Deere, August 1978

At the third national agricultural mechanisation conference in Beijing, 1978, Hua Guofeng, Ye Jianying, Deng Xiaoping and Li Xiannian, along with other party and state leaders, received conference participants. Xiang Nan is sixth from left in the front row of standing delegates

chairman of the CPC and premier, as well as Vice-Premier Li Xiannian and other leaders paid very serious attention to the study report, and set up a special meeting with Xiang Nan in Zhongnanhai to hear his account.

Xiang Nan prepared painstakingly for his report. He methodically recounted the processes involved in the visit to the US, and showed films of the visit, allowing the leaders to see for the very first time and to feel just how modern the country was. His presentation of the advanced state of American agriculture left especially deep impressions.

Xiang Nan went so far as to say to Hua Guofeng: "We have to shrink 'three great distinctions' [between town and country, between industry and agriculture, and between physical and mental work], but those three distinctions are far smaller in the US than they are in China." It required considerable courage, at that moment, to introduce the top-ranked capitalist country in admiring tones, and to voice recognition of his own country's backwardness. Xiang Nan's remarks left Hua Guofeng lost in thought, but he warned Xiang Nan not to speak this way to others lower down in the ranks.

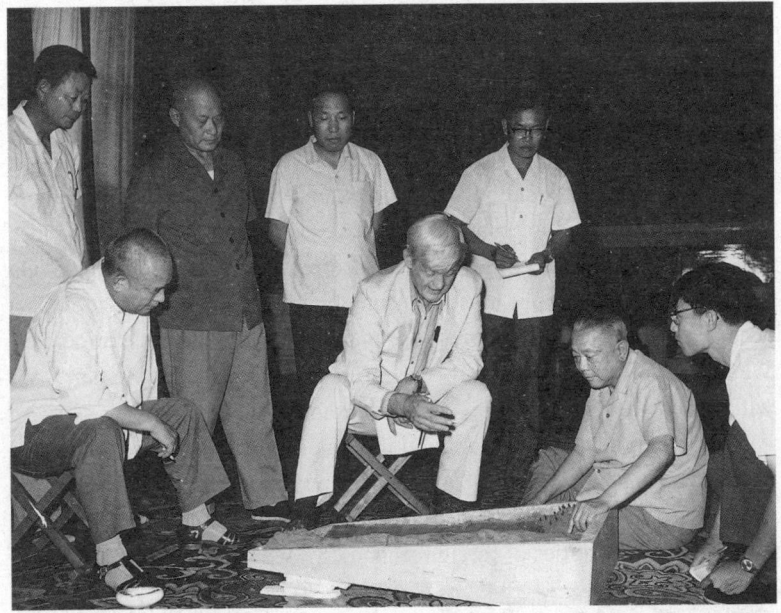

Xiang Nan accompanies vice-premiers Li Xiannian and Yu Qiuli during a meeting with William Hinton, 1978

In April 1978, Xiang Nan, in charge of agricultural mechanisation within the first ministry of machine building, led another delegation abroad, this time to study the agricultural equipment industry in Italy, France, the UK and Denmark.

Concluding that tour after a month, Xiang Nan sent his report to the party centre and the state council. In addition to reporting on the trip before the central leadership, Xiang Nan presented a report to various government administrators and provincial-level officials at the central party school.

Xiang Nan analysed in specific terms the development of agriculture in the US and each of the European countries he had visited. In his view, the development of modern socialist agriculture in China had to be viewed from four angles.

First, agriculture, forestry and animal husbandry were all important, with animal husbandry holding pride of place. As Xiang Nan put it: "We must not focus solely on planting and growing grain while ignoring husbandry and forestry."

Second, a relatively clear economic demarcation of agriculture was required. Xiang Nan noted: "If we fail to consider rational economic definitions, this plot of land that should be devoted to wet rice cultivation will not plant rice; that field that should be planted to sugarcane will not be; cotton will not be sown in fields best planted with cotton; land best suited for peanut production will be planted with wheat – none of these lands will be utilised to their full potential." He hammered home the idea that "taking grain as the key link" was incorrect, pointing out sharply: "On this question, we simply must free our thinking, mobilise our tools, act according to varying local conditions and respect the objective principles. We must avoid giving out confused orders and mandates. If we don't, we will be punished by those very objective principles."

Third, a high level of agricultural mechanisation and specialisation was needed. Xiang Nan warned: "We cannot buy modernisation in order to modernise. We can only rely on ourselves to bring about modernity. As we import major quantities of foreign technology, we must keep our heads."

Xiang Nan and his American friend William Hinton visit a state farm on the outskirts of Beijing, 1978

Fourth, modern science and technology must be applied to agricultural production. Xiang Nan argued that the nation had to adopt a series of major policies in the political realm, in economics, in science and in technology in support of agriculture, protecting the farmers' power to manage their own affairs while massively improving labour productivity.

At a time when the movement to learn from the Dazhai 'production brigade in agriculture' was still flourishing and the debate over the idea that 'experience is the sole criterion of truth' had not yet ended, Xiang Nan's ringing positive evaluation of agricultural modernisation in capitalist countries, and his re-thinking of decades-old problems of China's agricultural development, unquestionably raised a number of major political perils.

In September 1980, in Beijing, the United Nations Industrial Development Organisation (UNIDO) convened a conference on exchanges and cooperation in the development of agricultural mechanisation. It was China's first international conference on that subject. The more than 90 delegates from 35 nations and regions exhibited high interest in the development of such mechanisation in China.

Xiang Nan leads a delegation to Denmark, 1978

A report in a Danish newspaper on the visit of Xiang Nan's delegation, 1978

At the conference, Xiang Nan presented an address entitled 'The Way Forward for China's Agricultural Mechanisation', frankly discussing with the foreign participants the great difficulties and challenges facing China. He pointed out: "Our nation has urgent hopes of quickly reforming our agricultural backwardness and our lack of experience with reality, and in the past we fell into the errors of excessive speed and inflated targets. We raised the slogan of realising agricultural modernisation by 1980. But actual practice has shown such slogans to be out of touch with reality and impossible to carry out. Agricultural mechanisation involves government agencies not only in agriculture but in industry, transportation, finance and education. We cannot approach it as a military operation, with any one of them leading all the rest. It ultimately depends on the pace of development of industry and transportation; on the speed of advance in the rural economy and in socialist enterprise; on the extension of agro-technical training; on credit levels and expenditures provided by the state; and, finally, on the speed with which the agricultural machinery sector and science and technology themselves develop."

Xiang Nan during his agricultural mechanisation study tour in France, 1978

Xiang Nan (front row, wearing hat) leads his delegation on a visit to a cattle farm in France's Aquitaine region

Xiang Nan leads a Chinese agriculture and agricultural mechanisation delegation to observe French animal husbandry, at a cattle farm in the Aquitaine region

A Path-breaker in the Liberation of Thinking

Xiang Nan and the Chinese agricultural mechanisation delegation inspect farm machinery in France, 1978

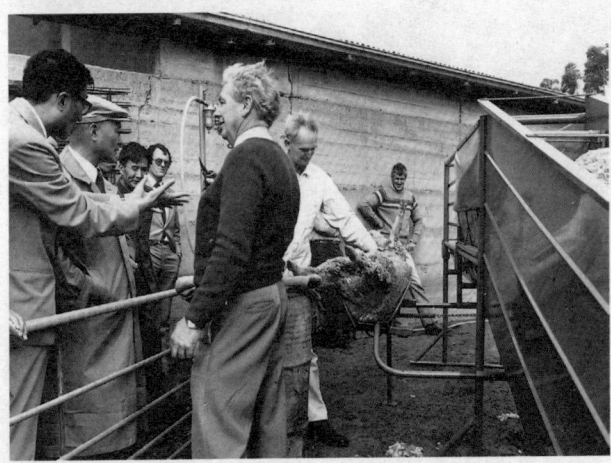

Xiang Nan observes farm machinery in Italy, 1978

Visiting Singapore in 1979, Xiang Nan talks with Goh Chok Tong, who would later become Singapore's prime minister

Xiang Nan inspects farm machinery in Australia, 1979

A Path-breaker in the Liberation of Thinking

During his sojourn at the ministry of agricultural machine-building, Xiang Nan and Hua Guofeng with the American friendly personages Erwin Engst (far left) and Joan Hinton (far right), November 1991

Xiang Nan enjoys a new year tea party in 1997 with former ministers of the ministry of agricultural machine-building. In the front row: Wu Shaowen (second from left), Yuan Chenglong (third from left), Yang Ligong (fifth from left), Xiang Nan (sixth from left) and He Guangyuan (seventh from left)

Chapter 24

Assigned as Ambassador to the Frontier with Deng Xiaoping's Support

After the third plenum of the 11th central committee in December 1978, the party centre confirmed that Fujian and Guangdong should take the lead in pursuing the policy of 'reform and opening up'. The two provinces were authorised to carry out 'special policies and flexible measures'. But two years passed, and 'leftist' ways of thinking were as deeply entrenched in Fujian as ever. The question of whether 'practice was the sole criterion of truth' had been debated at length but had not really advanced. The leading figures in the provincial party were not of one mind on implementing the agricultural reform policy that gave greater decision-making powers to individual farm households. Work on all sorts of tasks wavered back and forth without advancing. The chasm between the provincial situation and the overall design approved by the central authorities was huge, not to mention the 'one step ahead of the rest' role assigned to Fujian. The vast ranks of cadres in the province were dissatisfied. Some patriotic overseas Chinese whose families came from Fujian even

Xiang Nan in 1980

Assigned as Ambassador to the Frontier with Deng Xiaoping's Support

wrote to the central leadership, calling on them to send a powerful commander to Fujian to take charge.

In 1980, the party centre's secretariat reached a decision on the personnel problem in Fujian. Fujian was the native land of many overseas Chinese; it sat on the cutting edge of reform and opening up. The centre wanted to find a comrade who was a Fujian native, deeply familiar with local conditions, to go to the province and take up duties there. Although Hu Yaobang felt that Xiang Nan was a suitable candidate, Xiang had worked for years at the top level of the CYL, and it was a little problematic for Hu Yaobang to recommend Xiang Nan for the job before any other recommendations arose.

Later, however, Deng Xiaoping settled the matter with a few words: "I think Xiang Nan could do it."

Hu Yaobang and a few other members of the central secretariat sought out Xiang Nan for a chat. They told him what was on their minds. But Xiang Nan did not seem to show any special eagerness.

Wan Li, another central secretariat member, spoke to Xiang Nan. "The centre is considering sending a Fujianese highly familiar with conditions in

Hu Yaobang and Xiang Nan

Xiang Nan (front row, third from left) accompanying Vice-Premier Wulanfu (front row, fifth from right) meet African guests, 1980

Fujian to return to the province and take charge of the work there," he said. "I've sought you out to hear your thoughts on this."

Xiang Nan answered frankly. "There is no question that I'm a Fujianese," he said. "But I haven't worked in Fujian for decades, and I'm really not very well informed about conditions there."

Hearing Xiang Nan speak this way, several members of the central secretariat were temporarily dumbstruck.

Finally, Hu Yaobang broke the silence. He slapped his thigh and rose from the sofa, saying in a loud voice: "He's a Fujianese and he hasn't worked there – that's good! He'll be all the more able to maintain his detachment."

Xiang Nan used the month's interval before his departure to read large amounts of material relating to the situation in Fujian. On 14 January 1981, Xiang Nan formally became secretary of the standing committee of the Fujian provincial party committee, with full powers to conduct the work of the party committee. A year later, the party centre formally appointed him first secretary of the Fujian provincial party committee.

Assigned as Ambassador to the Frontier with Deng Xiaoping's Support

In 1982, the party centre appointed Xiang Nan first secretary of the Fujian provincial party committee and first political commissar of the provincial military district. This photo shows Xiang and Wang Zhixin in Fuzhou

Xiang Nan and his granddaughter Lianlian at play

Xiang Nan and his mother Wang Cunyu in Fuzhou

Chapter 25

The Most Urgent Task in Fujian is the Liberation of Thinking

On the first day of his new assignment, Xiang Nan happened upon a meeting of party secretaries from the local, city and county levels that had been called by the Fujian provincial party committee. He alighted from the train, fatigued from the long journey from Beijing, and went straight to the meeting.

At the meeting, Xiang Nan came to realise that, influenced by the provincial party committee's main leaders, localities all over the province were putting up fierce resistance to the agricultural reform policy of 'contracting agricultural production at the household', assigning fixed farm quota contracts to individual households and leaving the households free to engage in other activities, so long as they met their contracts. The new system was reviled as a form of 'dividing the land for individual work', a 'retreat' and a 'rightist deviation' that would inevitably slide onto the road to capitalism.

Without a liberation of thought itself, the strong development of productive forces was an impossibility. Xiang Nan realised deeply that the most pressing task facing Fujian was the emancipation of minds. Without that, no other problems would be worth talking about.

On Xiang Nan's seventh day in Fujian, on 20 January 1981, a provincial party congress convened. For the first time, Xiang Nan stood before delegates from the entire province, and offered an impromptu address entitled 'Speaking of the Emancipation of Minds'.

Xiang Nan pointed out that Fujian possessed eight important foundations needed for the building of the nation: forestry, animal husbandry, fishing, cash crops, light industry, foreign trade, science and technology, and as a critical location for the unification of the motherland. He then added: "From today's perspective, Fujian's advantages have not been very well brought into play and, as a result, provincial development has not been rapid. People are earning barely enough to provide themselves with adequate clothing and food. To reach our goals, we must liberate our thinking, unstintingly rooting out the influences of 'leftist' thought."

Xiang Nan presented his remarks without a text, speaking every word, every sentence, straight from his heart.

"The central government decided to give Fujian even greater autonomy, and permission to implement special policies of greater flexibility. The province may use larger amounts of foreign capital, and develop its foreign trade, so as to make Fujian's economic development more dynamic and rapid than that of neighbouring provinces. But if our minds remain less emancipated than our neighbours', our economic liberalisation policies less resolute, and the measures we take less flexible, to the point that the things called for by the central authorities are treated flippantly and cannot be realised, how can we possibly 'enliven the economy' and do a decent job of building Fujian?

"I recommend that every district, every agency, every work unit thinks very hard about this. What is 'special' in our 'special policies'? Where lies the 'flexibility' in our 'flexible measures'?

"Eliminating the influences of 'left' thinking must rest mainly with party committees at both the provincial and local levels, including all the departments, commissions, offices and bureaus within the provincial party and the provincial government. The most crucial unit is the standing committee of the provincial party committee. At this conference, a number of comrades have asked: are 'leftist' errors still to be found within the provincial party committee? If they are, how are they manifested? On these questions, our provincial party committee must take the initiative and conduct rigorous criticism and self-criticism. According to the mandate from the party centre, we must come up with answers to these questions within two months."

Finally, Xiang Nan spoke of his own personal feelings and hopes for Fujian. "The waters of Fujian are so magnificent. Our mountains are so luxuriant. For Fujian to take flight quickly, all will depend on whether or not our minds are emancipated."

The Most Urgent Task in Fujian is the Liberation of Thinking

Xiang Nan's speech was, in essence, an oath of mental emancipation, opening the gates to a spring flood surging into the hearts of the conference delegates.

In the debates that followed, many delegates responded that Xiang Nan's address had powerfully struck a chord; it had been many years since Fujian had heard a report as fine as this.

The delegates put forward three requests and hopes. First, they hoped that the standing committee of the provincial party committee would set an example in implementing the spirit of Xiang Nan's speech, offering a model for others to follow. Second, nearly all delegates wished for the transcription of Xiang Nan's extemporaneous remarks to be distributed in full throughout the ranks of the party at all levels. And third, they asked that the documentary films of Xiang Nan's travels abroad be shown widely.

On 14 May 1981, the general office of the party central committee distributed Xiang Nan's speech to the provinces and to the military, with this special notation: "On 20 January last year, comrade Xiang Nan made a speech entitled 'Speaking of the Emancipation of Minds' at a provincial party congress session. The speech was personally prepared by this leading cadre, and was not simply a recitation of remarks prepared by secretarial staff. This speech is rooted in reality. It raises questions and it resolves them. It is clear and concise, vivid and lively. It is devoid of formulaic, empty prose. We recommend that you read it."

Chapter 26

Taking up the Responsibility System for Agrarian Production, as a Breakthrough Tool

After the provincial party congress, to get a better sense of conditions in Fujian, Xiang Nan set out on a special excursion, travelling very light, to have a look at the entire province.

In Putian, Xiang Nan observed that, because the provincial party committee had not turned its attention to the responsibility system in farm production, most commune residents were troubled. They wanted to start spring planting quickly, but some of the land that needed ploughing was still covered with rice stubble from the previous harvest. Many of the longan tree roots were still exposed, and no one was available to spread manure.

Xiang Nan, accompanied by the party secretary of Zhangpu county Huang Buxiang (far right) and others, observe the Fujian Zhangpu shrimp farming operation, January 1981

Taking up the Responsibility System for Agrarian Production, as a Breakthrough Tool

Xiang Nan visits the grassroots to study the household contract responsibility system, 1981

Everyone who talked with Xiang Nan naturally brought up the problem that, at both the provincial and local level, some responsible officials sternly refused to allow use of the household contracting responsibility system and put up stern resistance to it. Xiang Nan replied: "For many years, our cadres were fearless. But one accusation of 'rightism', one hint that they are taking the capitalist road, and they tremble, terrified by a single bad mention. The cadres are afraid that if they have any problems, in the end their careers will suffer. How do they have time to worry about whether the people have enough to eat? What is wrong with the household contracting system? What's wrong with dividing up the land for individuals to work on their own? As long as they increase production and can pull in a rich harvest, if the people support it, let them do it!"

The attending local and country leaders were awestruck.

Back in 1962 at the Beidaihe conference, a fierce debate had broken out among the highest leaders of the party over the question of a responsibility system for the land and a system of contracting with individual households. As a result, Deng Zihui, the vice-premier who at the time headed the party's central rural work department in overall charge of rural work, left his post in despair. Chen Yun was called an 'old rightist' because he had supported small-scale experiments with the household contracting system, and was shoved aside. After that, for a long time the household contract system and the responsibility system remained untouchable territory.

In 1978, China's reforms started in the rural sector. These reforms began with the introduction of 'responsibility fields' and the contracting-out of farm lands. Xiang Nan was certain that a contract system that linked remuneration to output would bring deep changes. The first thing he intended to do when he arrived in Fujian was expand the household contract responsibility system.

At that time, the central leadership did not have a fixed schedule for the enactment of the household contract responsibility system. Their Document No. 75 had said that remote mountain districts and the most impoverished and backward districts could proceed with either of two forms of the household responsibility system, each providing for individual household retention of surplus production after fulfilment of required quotas owed to the state and the collective.

Xiang Nan observes conditions in the Fuzhou suburbs, 1982

Taking up the Responsibility System for Agrarian Production, as a Breakthrough Tool

As soon as Xiang Nan reached Fujian, he resolved to quickly implement the 'household contract responsibility system'. This unquestionably took political courage. Above all, the thinking processes of the senior leadership in Fujian had still not been freed and remained rooted in 'leftist' patterns of thought. One important leader said publicly at a big meeting: "I will cancel the party membership of anyone who even mentions the household responsibility system."

"What is there to fear from the household responsibility system?" Xiang Nan asked with a mild expression on his face. But his words were hard: "I am telling you: these household responsibility systems are not individual farming. We are now carrying out a variety of different forms of production responsibility systems, but we have not altered the ownership system. Even if they did constitute individual farming, how can you call that capitalism? In the past we all 'ate from the big pot' together, talking big and saying nice things about 'collectivisation' and speaking ill of life in the bad old days. That was not communism, and it wasn't socialism. It didn't have the attributes of capitalism or feudalism either. Nor was it like the ancient 'slave society'. It was more like the 'primitive communism' stage of earliest human history, when several hundred people would surround a single deer, all pursuing it together, while hollering to each other. That was how the deer was taken. Now think about that and imagine that that was how the lunch we enjoyed today had been provided. If that one deer had not been taken, we would all be going hungry. That was how society under primitive communism worked. Do we want to drag today's economy back to those ancient times? That is not progress – it is a retreat."

From what he saw and heard as he travelled, Xiang Nan decided that bearing down on the production responsibility system would be a real breakthrough for reform and opening up in Fujian. Soon after returning to Fuzhou from southern Fujian, he made time to go to the offices of *Fujian Daily*, where he earnestly made his case. "From now on, when the provincial party committee meets, except for the time when personnel matters are being discussed, you senior editors of *Fujian Daily* may attend, so that you can more quickly come to understand both the spirit that now animates the party centre and the intentions of the provincial party committee.

"You need to understand that focusing on the agricultural responsibility system is a top publicity priority at present. You need to stimulate broad-scale social discussion of it. When every household knows about the responsibility system, that will ignite a powerful moving force." In his discussions with the leaders of the newspaper, Xiang made himself very clear: "This agricultural production we are talking about is not the agriculture of the old 'take grain as the key link' days. This is 'big agriculture', embracing farming, forestry, animal husbandry, sideline occupations and fisheries." Xiang Nan instructed the journalists to produce an editorial focused on carrying out the agricultural responsibility system, under the title 'Realisation of the Agricultural Responsibility System Can Brook No Delay', and asked that the editorial appear on the first day of the lunar new year.

When the editorial was drafted, Xiang Nan read it with a critical eye, and took up his pen to make a number of improvements. After Xiang personally revised it, the stance of the editorial was even clearer and more persuasive. On the first day of the lunar new year, the editorial 'Realisation of the Agricultural Responsibility System Can Brook No Delay' appeared in the most prominent position in the newspaper.

According to Xiang Nan's instruction, the second section of *Fujian Daily* that day reprinted, in an equally conspicuous spot, a *People's Daily* article published a few days earlier. This article, entitled 'The Great Power of Attraction', reported at length on the major changes that occurred when Anhui, Henan and Shandong introduced the responsibility system. Xiang Nan personally expressed his own very clear viewpoint in an editor's note that was in the nature both of a guiding document and a call to action. Everyone could therefore see, in the black and white of a newspaper article, the clear attitude

Xiang Nan takes part in tree-planting at the Fujian forest park, 1982

and powerful resolve of the provincial party committee with respect to the agricultural responsibility system.

On 6 February 1981, the Fujian provincial communist party committee issued the *Announcement Regarding the Firm-handed Implementation of the Responsibility System*. The document called on leaders at every level to gather their forces, act in accordance with local conditions and implement the system with the maximum speed.

On the evening of 10 February, the provincial party committee and the provincial government jointly called a province-wide telephone conference to discuss implementation of the new system. Each locality, city and county was to pay strict attention to the attitude of the provincial leadership and get to work.

During the telephone conference, problem after problem came up. The local party committee from Jianyang said: "Formerly, the first party secretary told us not to set up the household guarantee system. Now, you are telling us to put that very system into effect with all our energies. Whom are we supposed to listen to, the first secretary or the 'standing secretary' in charge of day-to-day work?"

This was a very sharp question, and Xiang Nan had to respond. His reply was clever: "Do not pay attention to the first secretary. Do not pay attention to the 'standing secretary' either. Pay attention to the party centre."

On 21 February, at a conference of heads of government agriculture bureaus from throughout the province, Xiang Nan nailed the essential point. "For many years, we have lived under a system of 'You set me to rights, I set you to rights'. You have said: 'Class struggle gets things done.' I say: 'Not necessarily.' On agricultural issues, to the contrary, it is the responsibility system that gets things done. Everyone, just get going – no problem."

Someone in the room raised his voice suddenly: "What happens if we're wrong. If we can't say that the responsibility system is capitalism, just what are we supposed to say?" That set off a big debate in the hall. Someone else who had many doubts pinned Xiang Nan with a fixed stare and asked Xiang to come out with a clear response.

Xiang Nan said in a booming voice: "You are not responsible for mistakes; I am. The party centre is. You say this is capitalism: have you ever seen capitalism? What is capitalism like? Eating from the big iron pot, egalitarianism – is that what you call communism? Have you looked at the history of society's evolution? That is not communism, it is not socialism, it isn't even capitalism or feudalism! What you're talking about is nothing more than primitive communism, the earliest stage of human organisation. You tell me, then: what kind of work does not have a responsibility system? Running a newspaper, editing, working as a shop clerk – these occupations do not have a responsibility system? A worker firmly runs his machine. A driver drives his car. How can you say these occupations have no responsibility system? Why is it that you don't accuse that driver in his vehicle of 'going it alone'? And you try to tell us that farmers planting their fields are 'going it alone'? Marx never said anything of the kind. If we dredge this question up yet again, we will drag the farmers into poverty and drag the nation into collapse."

In a ringing voice, Xiang Nan expressed his own stance: "Implementing the agricultural production responsibility system must happen now. There must be no delay!"

Xiang Nan accompanies Du Runsheng, director of the central research institute on rural policy, and Du's team on an inspection of rural villages in Fujian, 1983

In spite of all this, many cadres still had misgivings. They worried that policies could change. This year's policies might only last a year; permissions once granted could be cancelled at any time. In the face of thinking like this, Xiang Nan demanded that the provincial party committee and the provincial government put forward explicit regulations, in black and white. The regulations were sent to the provincial people's congress, where they passed after debate and were put into effect.

In the space of only a few months after Xiang Nan took up his duties, the household responsibility system was put fully into effect throughout the province in time for the spring planting season.

Kim Il Sung, secretary of the Korean Workers' Party (front row, fifth from right) receives a delegation from China's NPC. In the front row, fourth from left, is Xi Zhongxun. Xiang Nan is in the front row, fourth from right. Third from left is Timur Dawamat, director of Xinjiang's standing committee. In the second row, third from left, is Gao Dengbang, deputy secretary general of the standing committee of the NPC

Chapter 27

'Making an SEZ is Imperative'

In October 1980, the state council formally approved the establishment of an SEZ in Xiamen. Three months later, when Xiang Nan took up his position in Fujian, the work of setting up the SEZ was still a blank slate.

On 11 March 1981, at a conference of cadres reporting directly to provincial-level authority, Xiang Nan presented a carefully designed address entitled 'It is not acceptable to fail to undertake the Xiamen SEZ'. He called on everyone in the province, at high levels and low, to get behind the project.

Xiang Nan speaks at a meeting of Guangdong and Fujian, convened by the party centre

Xiang Nan (second from left), Vice-Premier Gu Mu (fourth from left) and Fujian Vice-Governor Zhang Yi (third from left) visit Xiahua Electric

In June of the same year, the party centre and the state council convened a meeting in Beijing to discuss Guangdong, Fujian and the work of SEZs. In his remarks to the meeting, Xiang Nan came directly to the point with a number of opinions:

Number one: just how 'special' are 'special policies'? Under present circumstances, Fujian cannot match Guangdong when it comes to recruiting capital from overseas Chinese and foreign investors, much less compare with Hong Kong or Singapore. For that reason, Fujian should receive even greater preferential conditions than those prevailing in Guangdong, Hong Kong or Singapore, and it should benefit from policies even more strongly supportive of recruitment of external investment. "To put it in concrete terms, we and foreign investors both benefit. We want to do this. The foreigners will benefit. Even if our side is not profitable, it causes us no harm. We want to do this. The foreigners will benefit. We might take a bit of a loss, but we can deal with our unemployment problems this way. We want to do this. We ask the state council to give its approval in principle." This was the first time Xiang Nan raised the strategic argument known as the 'three want-to-do's'.

Number two: we must enlarge autonomy at the local level. Since the centre cannot presently provide greater financial support to the two provinces, it will be crucial to enact genuinely 'special policies' that really are 'special', moving some powers downward to local levels. We can explore how to give the 'three authorities' to Fujian under the prerequisites articulated in the centre's 'six unifications' policy. Those three authorities are personnel powers, financial authority and local law-making authority. The structuring of organisations below the provincial level, and their personnel and equipment matters, should be decided by the provincial party committee and the provincial government on the basis of need. Fujian and Guangdong must be permitted to recruit technical talent abroad, and they must have autonomy on matters of finance, taxation, banking, credit, trade, customs, prices and wages. This includes the authority to set up provincial banks. The two provinces must also be able to enact single-issue laws, simply reporting to the central authorities on the actions they have taken.

At this central work conference, Xiang Nan went further, arguing: "At present, before the two provinces have made major strides forward,

An NPC delegation led by Xi Zhongxun, with Xiang Nan and Timur Dawamat as deputy leaders, view the Yalu river while on a mission to North Korea, 1982

no one should be overly concerned that 'special policies' are going to be 'too flexible'. On the contrary, what is necessary is to awaken the two provinces. The special policies and flexible measures that the centre has granted to you are a kind of weapon: why are you afraid of special policies? Why are you intimidated by flexibility? Why, until today, have you not opened things up? The question of the hour is this: we must encourage our cadres to dare to venture forth, dare to take risks and dare to open things up. Making mistakes here and there is inevitable. You haven't forged ahead because you are still afraid of disorder, of committing errors. If you don't dare to take giant strides ahead, you will never gain experience!"

With Xiang Nan setting the pace, construction work on the Huli industrial district in Xiamen SEZ started formally on 15 October 1981.

When the time came to decide on a name for the special district, Huli processing district officially became known as Huli processing district of Xiamen SEZ, rather than the Xiamen Huli SEZ. Although this only changed a couple of words, the meaning of the change was profound. From the start, Xiang Nan and the others creating the SEZ had no intention of confining it to the 2.5 square kilometres of Huli; rather, they set their sights on the entire island of Xiamen.

Upon the arrival in Pyongyang of a special aircraft bearing China's NPC delegation, Korean children presented the delegation with flowers. Xiang Nan is in the back row, second from left. Third from left is Xi Zhongxun

Chapter 28

The Nation's First 10,000-Line Digital-Switching Telephone System

In 1980, a French businessman attempted to make a long-distance business phone call from Fuzhou to Paris. After two days and two nights, he was still not able to connect. On the third day, furious, he left China. Before he departed, he said, with no attempt at courtesy, something like this: "You do not understand efficiency. You have no concept of time."

The basic infrastructure in Fujian was backward, and was already severely hampering economic development. At that time, the entire annual revenue of the province only came to Rmb100m, not nearly enough to pay for the many recommended infrastructure improvements. Xiang Nan said: "Without infrastructure measures, we cannot build the environment needed for 'opening up'. We are going to have to create our own miracle."

Xiang Nan supported the provincial posts and telecommunications bureau's importation of a set of equipment for a 10,000-line digital switching telephone system to be installed in Fuzhou, in order to improve telecommunications in the provincial capital. The posts and telecommunications bureau's choice of a foreign company capable of building the necessary advanced equipment took 13 months and 17 rounds of negotiations with a total of eight foreign companies. In the end, the Japanese firm Fujitsu's FETEX-150 digital switch was deemed satisfactory.

This Fuzhou telecommunications switch was a first-generation system, at a time when international usage had reached the fourth generation. Fujitsu's fourth-generation telecommunications equipment had just entered into testing. Xiang Nan's view was that, while it might entail some risk, Fuzhou could provide Fujitsu with a test base. And thus the cost of introducing a complete set of 10,000-line digital switching telecommunications equipment could be far lower than normal list prices.

The Nation's First 10,000-Line Digital-Switching Telephone System

In November 1982, Fuzhou became the first Chinese city to operate a 10,000-line digital switching telephone system. Making a direct international call now took 20-30 seconds. In one night, Fuzhou's telecommunications had leapfrogged several technological generations. Its 'aim high/leap ahead/ one giant step to the front rank' example was a national sensation. At that time, the number of large and medium-sized Chinese cities where direct international calling was possible could be counted on a person's fingers. In a number of developed countries and regions such as Singapore and Hong Kong, telecommunications technologies had not yet reached the Fuzhou standard. Thus the leapfrogging manner of Fuzhou's telecommunications engineering aroused strong interest.

Following that, Xiamen also brought in a complete 10,000-line digital switching system, guaranteeing smooth connections and superior sound quality. Three months after the system went into operation, the number of deals signed by the zone with foreign businesses had doubled.

In February 1983, Xi Zhongxun, a secretary in the central party secretariat, came to Fujian on an inspection tour, and Xiang Nan invited him to view the Fuzhou digital phone system. Xi heartily approved, and recommended to Guangdong province that it, too, should speedily adopt such a system. Thus, Guangdong was roughly two years behind Fujian in installing a digital switching telephone system. Later on, all China's provinces and major cities followed Fujian's example, and began setting up their own digital phone systems.

Chapter 29

Using Foreign Investment as Wings for the SEZ's Smooth Takeoff

I f Xiamen wanted to build an SEZ, not having an airport was unthinkable. At the first operations meeting of the Xiamen SEZ management committee, Xiang Nan put it clearly: "No airport, no SEZ. We must make the decision to build an airport. Now that we are creating an SEZ and increasing our openness to the outside world, we must fly outward."

Xiang Nan, guided by a senior representative from Fujian Shipping Company, visits the China shipping industry exhibition. Xiang Nan had great hopes for shipbuilding in Fujian. Fujian was the first province to look for foreign loans, and actively supported the growth of the shipbuilding industry in the province

Using Foreign Investment as Wings for the SEZ's Smooth Takeoff

In 1981, Fujian province's commitment of its own funds for the expansion of the airport at Fuzhou was a rarity. However, the matter of a Xiamen airport was not a funding issue; the question was whether such an airport could be included in the economic plan. Launching the Xiamen airport project initially ran into difficulty when the military firmly rejected it. Its argument was that Xiamen was too close to Taiwan, within sight of the islands of Little Jinmen and Big Jinmen that lay under Taiwan control; how could a civilian aviation airfield possibly be built?

The commander-in-chief or the PLA air force, Zhang Tingfa, was a Fujianese. Xiang Nan first sought him out and secured his agreement. Commander Zhang said: "Those opposing a Xiamen airport are not just a couple of air force members; the opposition ranges all the way to the central military commission and the general staff department of the PLA. I can't simply snap my fingers and change their minds. You need to create a team to work on them." Xiang Nan could only lead a team from the provincial party committee and the provincial government up to Beijing to set to work. The military's attitude was still unyielding: "If Xiamen builds an airport like this, if it falls under artillery bombardment from Jinmen, a couple of direct hits will obliterate your expensive investment, and that will be that."

In September 1982, attending the 12th CPC congress, Xiang Nan was elected as a member of the CPC central committee. Here, Xiang Nan casts his vote at the 12th congress

"I'm afraid such talk is wrong," Xiang Nan replied forthrightly, if a little impolitely. "Aren't you failing to see that Jinmen's own airfield is within range of our artillery? Militarily, who fears whom? Is Taiwan afraid of us, or are we afraid of Taiwan?"

"Needless to say, Taiwan is afraid of us," the generals replied, unwilling to be outshone.

"Well, if Taiwan fearlessly builds an airfield on their front line, why are we still fearful? The flight of Chiang Kai-shek and Chiang Ching-kuo to Taiwan proved their defeat and our victory. We defeated millions of KMT troops; what is so imposing about the tiny island of Taiwan? To this day, Chiang Ching-kuo is afraid to adopt the 'three connections [postal, commercial or air transport links].''

The generals opposing construction of a Xiamen airport were silent for a time, and could not come up with a refutation. In the end, the military gave the green light to the proposed Xiamen airport.

But where would the funds come from?

Xiang Nan sought out Li Xiannian, vice-chairman of the CPC and vice-

Xiang Nan accompanies CPC General Secretary Hu Yaobang on an inspection of construction work at the port of Xiamen, 1982

premier. They talked for more than half a day. Xiang's sole purpose was to struggle for the central government's assistance.

Li Xiannian listened carefully for half a day. Finally, he said: "Comrade Xiang Nan, what you say makes sense, and we should support you. But, to tell you frankly, we have an old saying: 'Just for money, there is no way, but for life itself, there is a way'." Li Xiannian smiled wordlessly.

Xiang Nan thought of Deng Xiaoping's earlier discussion with Xi Zhongxun. "The SEZ needs funding, but there is none. You have to carve your own bloody path." Xiang Nan made up his mind: he would not ask the central authorities for funds. He would figure out his own ways to solve the funding problem.

At a meeting of the standing committee of the provincial party committee, Xiang Nan put it this way. "We have to build a Xiamen airport. But under present circumstances, with the central government unable to invest in the project, we have to make use of the special policies we have been granted, and look for foreign loans to fund the airport."

Fujian already had some precedents for recruiting foreign loans. The Huafu Company, under provincial government control, had borrowed from Bank of America to buy boats, assemble ships' crews and open direct maritime service between Fujian and Hong Kong. Discussions on loans were under way with Kuwait, led by Fujian Vice-Governor Zhang Yi. This was the first time foreign loans were to be used in a basic infrastructure programme. Xiang Nan was gratified that his proposal to use foreign loans in this way was approved by the provincial party standing committee without objection.

At that time, all of the Gulf states were offering foreign loans. The state import and export commission included Xiamen airport in a list of projects it was discussing with Kuwait.

Xiang Nan and CPC General Secretary Hu Yaobang look out towards the Taiwan Strait, 1982

On 23 October 1983, the first airport constructed with foreign investment – Xiamen international airport – was inaugurated. The photo shows Xiang Nan (third from right) with Ye Fei, vice-chairman of the standing committee of the NPC (third from left) and Yang Chengwu, commander of Fuzhou military district (second from left) at the inaugural ribbon-cutting ceremony

Agreement was quickly reached with the Kuwaitis. A loan of US$2.2bn, at 3.3% annual interest, was made to Fujian province for the construction of Xiamen airport.

Given China's capacity for building such projects, the Xiamen airport programme was likely to take three or even four years. After he heard the briefing by Shen Tu, the head of China's civil aviation bureau, he said: "Well, then, what shall we do? The SEZ is supposed to wait another three or four years. Let me tell you; by that time, I may no longer even be in Fujian. Do you think we can get the project done within a year?"

"Impossible," replied Shen Tu, whose own experiences had left him cautious.

In October 1981, the Minjiang hydroelectric engineering bureau, a Fujian concern, had sent to Xiang Nan a do-or-die pledge, in the spirit of 'burning their boats, with their backs to the wall', to build the main runway within one year, and guaranteed the opening of aviation routes by 1983.

The attention of the leadership brought about effective changes in the way things were done, and the airport construction project moved ahead with unusual speed. Ground-breaking took place on 10 January 1982, and by the year's end the main runway was completed, a model of rapid domestic construction of a concrete airport runway within the space of a single year.

At 10.03am on 29 July 1983, a Trident passenger jet on a test flight landed smoothly on the main runway at Xiamen airport. The head of the Shanghai civil aviation bureau, Yuan Taoyuan, who led the test flight crew, stepped vigorously from the plane and said with unconcealed excitement: "The test flight was very successful. The airport has been built quickly and well, and it complies completely with international airport standards!"

From the formal start of construction until completion, the Xiamen airport project took only eight-and-a-half-months (not counting preliminary engineering). Few could have imagined such speed.

Xiang Nan (front row, right) and CPC General Secretary Hu Yaobang (front row, second from right) visit the Matiao hydroelectric station in Yongchun county, November 1982. Li Peng, vice-minister of water conservancy and electric power, is third from right in the front row

Xiang Nan (second from left) and Fujian Vice-Governor Zhang Yi (left) meet with Prince Faisal, head of the Kuwait Arab Economic Development Fund, on the occasion of the opening of commercial air services from Xiamen international airport, 21 October 1983

In October 1983, prior to the determination of air routes from Xiamen airport, Xiang Nan sent a telegram of invitation to Prince Faisal of Kuwait to participate in the formal ceremonies inaugurating the new air routes. The prince still could not believe it. He sent the following interesting reply to Xiang Nan: "Mr Xiang, you are a man of humour. I hope you will tell me definitively when the airport can be completed."

On 21 October, 1,000 Chinese and international invited guests came to witness ceremonies marking the inauguration of scheduled services from Xiamen. A Singapore Boeing 737 landed gently, and the hangar doors opened. Xiang Nan, accompanied by the vice-chairman of the standing committee of the NPC Ye Fei and Kuwait's Prince Faisal, stepped briskly down the staircase, amid fluttering flags and the deafening sound of gongs and drums. A sparkling new airport stood before them.

Xiamen SEZ finally had the wings it needed to take flight.

Using Foreign Investment as Wings for the SEZ's Smooth Takeoff

Xiang Nan (second from right) accompanyies President Li Xiannian (far right) on a visit to Xiamen, viewing the burial place of Tan Kah Kee, the renowned Fujianese entrepreneur, educator and philanthropist, 1983

Chapter 30

Establishing the First Sino-Foreign Joint Venture Company

Until the early 1980s, Fujian, on the front line of maritime defence, had experienced no major development for 30 years. Central government investment in Fujian over that period constituted just 0.8% of total national investment, and not a single large or medium-scale project built under national government regulations was located in the province. In terms of both its economic foundations and the speed of its economic development, Fujian lagged far behind other provinces, and it could not even begin to be compared with Guangdong.

When Xiang Nan first arrived in Fujian, he proposed that the 2.5 square kilometre SEZ authorised for Xiamen by the central authorities be expanded to encompass the entire island. Hu Yaobang made clear that the zone was to be limited to 2.5 square kilometres. The photo shows Hu Yaobang (second from right) and Xiang Nan receiving the report of Xiamen Party Secretary Lu Zifen (right) on the construction situation in the zone, 1982

Establishing the First Sino-Foreign Joint Venture Company

On 1 July 1979, the *Law of the PRC on Sino-Foreign Joint Venture Enterprises* was approved. From that date until the end of 1979, six projects nationwide received approval, with foreign capital totalling US$8.1m. Clearly, at the very outset, joint ventures faced major risks. In order to reform Fujian and place it at the front of the line, Xiang Nan led the whole province in making use of the 'special policies and flexible measures' that the central authorities had granted to Fujian to forge its own path, starting with major infrastructure facilities in order to attract increased investment.

In June 1981, Fujian Hitachi Television, with joint investment by Fujian and the Japanese company Hitachi, formally started production. This was the first Sino-foreign joint venture firm registered in China. Although China had established the joint venture law by then, the accompanying implementing regulations were another matter. The fog of 'leftist' thinking still hung heavily. Elsewhere in society, this brand-new development encountered a mixed reception. From the level of central authorities down to the localities, all sorts of different opinions emerged. One vice-premier called the Fujian Hitachi joint venture a "factory with a colonialist nature". Saddled with this kind of ugly labelling, the debate over Fujian Hitachi raised intense national concern.

Facing enormous pressures and numerous difficulties, Xiang Nan recalled Deng Xiaoping. Deng's message, "On the SEZs, I have made it clear: there are to be no debates", became Xiang Nan's spiritual motivation in dealing with endless difficulties and obstacles. Using the 'no debates' method, he unhesitatingly threw his strongest support to Fujian Hitachi.

On 2 November 1982, Hu Yaobang, general secretary of the CPC, came to Fujian on an inspection visit. With him on his team were Hu Qili, Gu Mu, Hao Jianxiu, Yang Dezhong, Li Peng and Jiang Zemin. During the visit, Hu Yaobang issued a series of instructions regarding Fujian's various projects, urging that the province serve as a pioneering example of economic construction. Hu also said: "Fujian has been very active in opening up, but at the moment it is not advancing very quickly and we cannot place all the blame on Fujian itself. The views of the relevant agencies at the centre are not united, and one cause of the problem is their insufficient support." Hu made a special address on the subject of Fujian Hitachi, pointing out: "Fujian Hitachi is a Sino-Japanese economic joint venture project. Even when it is not doing well, we have to stand firmly behind it and manage it well." Hu's remarks strengthened people's commitment to doing a good job with this joint venture enterprise, but they did not put an end to the continuing debate.

Xiang Nan and Australia's ambassador to China, Stephen Fitzgerald, visit the Luoxing pagoda outside Fuzhou, 1983

Xiang Nan with the Fujian poet and educator Liang Piyun (left) and Hong Kong industrialist Ko Bei Cheen in Fuzhou Forest Park, 1983

Both at the top, among some leading central figures, and at lower levels within and beyond the province, plenty of people were criticising Fujian Hitachi for 'treasonous activities', or for being a 'colonialist economy'. Seeing that neither Xiang Nan nor Zhang Yi, the provincial vice-governor responsible for external trade and investment, was willing to admit fault, some people went directly to the state planning commission and the state economic commission in an effort to block or completely paralyse the project. As a result, the state planning commission declined to accept Fujian Hitachi's production plans. Government agencies handling commerce, as well as agencies of the state administration of industry and commerce, notified Fujian Hitachi that any sales of television sets outside Fujian province would require official certificates of approval, or else they would be treated as smuggled goods.

In order to protect the achievements of reform and opening up introduced into Fujian Hitachi's production lines, Xiang pushed back forcefully without regard to his own career. Unbendingly, against immense pressure, he was determined not to let Fujian Hitachi succumb.

In 1984, at a meeting with the chairman of Hitachi Industries Corporation, Takahashi Toyokichi, Xiang Nan made his attitude clear: "The cooperation between Fujian and Hitachi is a success. We hope that it will last long into the future."

Xiang Nan took the cooperation between Fujian and Hitachi in jointly operating Fujian Hitachi as a milestone, and he set out to make Fujian-Japan cooperation in the field of electric tools a second milestone. He sought for Fujian and Hitachi to build broader and more comprehensive cooperation, establishing additional 'third milestones'. The Japanese side strongly concurred with Xiang Nan's view and expressed its determination to carry out fuller and wider-ranging cooperation with Fujian.

To carry out that cooperation, however, certain problems had to be resolved. Because Fujian Hitachi had been dealt a crippling blow by its exclusion from the government's economic plan, it could not gain access to foreign exchange with which to buy needed equipment sets and components. As a result, production could not be guaranteed, while masses of goods already produced remained in huge unsold inventories.

Xiang Nan was extremely concerned. He looked for ways to support

Xiang Nan meets with Cambodia's King Norodom Sihanouk in Fuzhou, 1983

alternative methods of dealing with the crisis. First, he arranged for the sale, in domestic currency, of several tens of thousands of colour television sets within Fujian's own boundaries. Then he calculated production costs in hard currency and arranged with the state planning commission to exchange the domestic currency for US$450m. This succeeded in reducing Fujian Hitachi's bloated inventories, speeded up the recovery of investment costs, stabilised the market and helped the plant to protect normal production operations. In addition, if helped to satisfy popular demand for televisions.

Virtually every large joint venture project ran into problems like this; Fujian Hitachi was not alone. In Xiamen, a joint venture between Xiamen Cigarette and Reynolds Tobacco of the US, set up to produce Camel cigarettes, brought in advanced machinery and technology. That led to an explosion of arguments. Some complained that the importation itself had been badly carried out. Others embellished the story by arguing that the

In 1985, Xiang Nan received a pioneering delegation of ambassadors to China from 37 countries, along with other diplomats and their spouses. He said proudly to them: 'For many years in the past, Fujian's rate of growth ranked 21st among China's 29 provinces, autonomous regions and centrally-administered municipalities. Last year, we advanced to third place. Our electronics industry originally ranked 18th. Last year it ranked sixth..." He made clear: 'Our policy of opening up is firm and will not waver. Fujian's gateway will only open more and more widely'

state ought to cancel any project elsewhere that resembled the Xiamen deal because, once China's doors were opened, no customs tax benefits resulted; or that the cigarettes to be produced by the joint venture company could not be sold overseas but could only be sold domestically, thus robbing China's own people of their funds.

At the critical moment, Xiang Nan stood up to say that carrying out the 'three imports and one compensation' business model posed no risks. "In the Xiamen Cigarette joint venture, we have spent no money. We have brought in advanced technology. We have brought in production equipment. We have acquired raw materials. Our workers have received training. The state has collected taxes. We have solved some of our unemployment challenges, and we have brought additional products to the market. What is wrong with any of that? What have we lost? Where are the risks? In a single year, Xiamen Cigarette has reached its projected demand level. It has mastered the technology. It is earning money. Where is the bad in that?"

Xiang Nan went further, saying: "Where in the world do we find perfection? If we insist on excessive demands, every activity will fail. I can guarantee that a project bears serious consideration, but if some problems appear, people should show some understanding instead of casting blame on others. We should praise and defend our cadres who have the pioneering creative spirit. They do their work in the face of risks. If someone makes a small mistake, we should treat him with good grace. We are lacking in experience when it comes to dealing with foreigners, and it is hard not to make errors from time to time. But as long as the intent is to serve the nation and not the individual, to serve the great enterprise of our party, and to develop our economy, we should treat those who make mistakes with sympathy, support them, and of course help them to set things to rights as quickly as possible."

Xiang Nan then said: "In the past, we had a song, *Forge the Trail, O Pioneers!* The words ran, 'Boom! Boom! Boom! We are the pathbreakers! Boom! Boom! Boom! We are the pioneers! We do not fear the mountain passes or heavy burdens!' Everyone should now have the spirit of those pathbreaking pioneers. Be the pioneers of reform and opening up."

Chapter 31

Thoroughly Redressing the Wrongful Cases Against Fujian's Underground Party Workers

After 1949, successive political movements created a vast number of cases of injustice. When Xiang Nan took up his post in Fujian, four years had already passed since the end of the 'Cultural Revolution', and the third plenum of the 11th central committee was already two years in the past. But a mountain of problems left by this historical legacy remained. Even old cadres who had participated in the land revolution and the war of resistance against Japan had fallen into prison. Some of these cases of false accusation had still not been settled, in spite of instructions from Hu Yaobang, Deng Xiaoping, Song Renqiong and others.

From the beginning of his service in Fujian, Xiang Nan had often spoken of the need to resolve these problems left over from history, and of the need to pay rapid attention to cadre policies and move smoothly and systematically to rectify cases of unjust accusation. He sternly ordered: do not simply settle old scores from the past, and do not go to excess in affixing blame. These situations are all the results of 'leftist' extremism.

In October 1981, at a meeting of the standing committee of the provincial party committee, Xiang Nan launched a strategy for 'firmly, thoroughly, speedily and compassionately' resolving problems bequeathed from history. Everything had to start from objective reality. The cases of Fujian CPC underground workers had to be investigated and cleared up, and their resolution had to be fair and fully public. To this end, the provincial party committee established a special 'office for the examination of problems regarding the party underground', and assigned someone with special responsibility for this work.

Beginning in 1982, Xiang Nan repeatedly convened the provincial party committee to discuss the resolution of these historical cases related to the party underground. Many underground comrades received treatment in line with the new policies. But because the numbers were so great, and because these cases dated from so long before, the situation was all the more complex. Some people refused to cooperate, and the whole process failed to live up to people's expectations.

In order to push this work forward, Xiang Nan sought help from universally respected senior figures such as Tan Zhenlin, Jiang Yizhen and Fan Shiren. Tan was a veteran comrade from the Jinggangshan days, who had worked in Fujian for a number of years and was very well acquainted with many of the questions arising from history. He had often said to the provincial party leadership: "Why haven't these false accusation cases been cleared up? Men such as Fu Bocui and Luo Ming, and that whole generation of revolutionaries, are in their 80s and 90s now. Why can't they be cleared and some work be found for them? Then there are other old comrades who spent three years in guerrilla war and served bravely in the war against Japan and the war of liberation. They acquitted themselves well, but because of a few words spoken in error in 1976, they were seized and remain in captivity. What kind of cadre policy is this?"

The restoration of honour to the falsely accused party cadres in Fujian caught the highest attention at the central level.

Xiang Nan and Tan Zhenlin (standing) hold a discussion with Fujian's veteran cadres

Thoroughly Redressing the Wrongful Cases Against Fujian's Underground Party Workers

The party's central secretariat sent an investigative team made up of members of the organisation department, the central discipline commission, the supreme people's procuratorate and other units to guide and further the work of rehabilitating underground party workers in Fujian who had been falsely accused.

In the spring of 1983, the province convened a seminar on the correct handling of the leftover cases relating to the Fujian party underground. Xiang Nan spoke, on behalf of the Fujian provincial party committee. He pointed out clearly: "The underground party of Fujian has a brilliant revolutionary history. We should restore its original revolutionary image. As for these questions bequeathed by history, we have to start with a proper overall strategy in order to resolve them in the most diligent manner." After much hard work, and with the support of the party centre and the provincial party committee, the 'three big cases' – involving the party underground in Fujian, Zhejiang and Jiangxi in the first instance, central Fujian in the second instance and western Fujian in the third instance – were redressed.

In 1982, Xiang Nan and Tan Zhenlin, vice-chairman of the standing committee of the NPC, visited old comrades in Fujian. In the front row, from left to right: Wu Hongxiang, He Minxue, Xiang Nan, Tan Zhenlin, Liu Yongsheng, Wei Jinshui and He Ruoren. In the second row, Wang Zhi (second from left), Ma Xingyuan (third from left), Lu Sheng (second from right). Chen Ting is in the third row, second from right

Another 405 cases of old cadres that had been unfairly handled after 1976 were thoroughly redressed. The cases of more than 6,000 individuals whose cases related to the party underground in Fujian were re-examined, and more than 4,000 former party underground workers had their party memberships restored.

Xiang Nan felt, however, that this was still not enough. Many of these underground party workers, as he saw it, were educated people who had suffered unfair treatment over long periods of time. Not only had their bodies suffered severe harm; many of them had lost their jobs and could not earn a living. Even those that did manage to work never received pay raises or promotions, and their lives were very difficult. To Xiang Nan's way of thinking, these people deserved better treatment. But, as in his work for rehabilitation of the falsely accused, Xiang Nan's efforts on this front faced many obstacles. He could only continue to sound the call on their behalf, time and time again.

This energetic effort by Xiang Nan ran into a spirited counterattack from many others. They promptly sent a secret letter of complaint to the centre. Central leaders, too, could not but take an interest in the matter. Xiang Nan excitedly told a central leadership delegation visiting Fujian: "A college student who worked in the party underground was unjustly treated and earns the same income now as someone who does odd jobs around the courtyard of an office. How can we dismiss this? What does 'respecting education' mean? What about 'honouring talent'? Does it really amount to that much to assist a person like this, who has suffered from injustice for half a lifetime, by elevating him three or four pay grades, up to rank number 20?"

On 10 March 1984, Jiang Yizhen, a former governor of Fujian and a member of the party's central advisory commission was in Fujian doing research. Xiang Nan and Jiang Yizhen shared ideas. Jiang drafted a *Recommendation on Some Questions of Policy Regarding Those Who Served in the Party Underground in Former KMT-controlled Areas of Southern Fujian*, and sent it to Hu Yaobang and other senior party leaders. Hu ordered the party's central organisation department to work urgently with the province to resolve this issue.

At about the time of Jiang Yizhen's report to Hu Yaobang, Xiang Nan

Xiang Nan with Xu Jimei, former vice-chairman of the Fujian Chinese people's political consultative conference and prior to that a responsible member of the party underground in central Fujian, pictured in the Temple of Heaven Park in Beijing

was seeking out Zhang Lian, Xu Jimei and others, one by one, to ask them to organise the old comrades who had once worked together in the Quanzhou area around a new enterprise. He urged them to make use of their many close connections to overseas Chinese, and to act as go-betweens in raising funds from overseas Chinese and foreign investors, thus opening up a new field for overseas Chinese contributions to economic development and construction.

When building the petrochemical base in Fujian, with adequate human resources in short supply, Xiang Nan remembered a onetime educated underground party worker from southwestern Fujian who had recently gained political rehabilitation. He wrote a personal letter to the deputy chairman of the provincial party committee, Zhang Weizi, saying: "The party organisation still owes it to these educated people who suffered such grievous harm to help them find appropriate work. Please mull this over with comrade Cheng Xu. Which cadres who did underground party work in western Fujian should now be put to good use? Please list them, specifying what work they could do. List them all. Now is the time to guide them in their functions. The party centre has by now created the necessary conditions for us to do this."

Xiang Nan: Champion of Reform in Fujian

Xiang Nan, coming out of the chaos of the 'Cultural Revolution', had personally known the physical effects of unjust treatment. With his generous and fearless spirit, and in the face of heavy pressure, but with the support of Hu Yaobang at the party centre, he thoroughly resolved the historical cases of injustice left behind in Fujian. In myriad ways he sought to arrange work for these long-suffering comrades, and to improve their compensation, acting on the principle that a person with skills deserved to put those skills to work. In doing so, Xiang Nan created in Fujian a more relaxed and harmonious political environment in which to pursue the great enterprise of reform and opening up.

Chapter 32

Implementing Policies for the Renowned Son of China and Entrepreneur Aw Boon Haw

Fujian is renowned as the native place of many overseas Chinese. In working to resolve matters left over from the past, and in particular to deal with the most sensitive issue concerning many overseas Chinese – properties that had been seized from them – Xiang Nan decided to face the problem head-on. In his words: "I recommend that the first party secretary himself grasp this question. Party members should take the lead. The provincial party must undertake a thorough investigation of all party secretaries and deputy party secretaries, mayors and special appointees,

Xiang Nan (third from left), Lin Kaiqin (third from right), Zhang Yumin (fourth from right) with others at Longyan, observe water and soil conservation work, and visit Chinese people of Taiwan origin living in Changting, 1983

During Xiang Nan's leadership of Fujian, the Taiwan Strait situation remained very serious. In April 1983, Xiang Nan (left), with Yang Chengwu, commander of the Fuzhou military region (right), met with Major Li Dawei, the KMT air force pilot who defected with his aircraft

as well as their children, to find out whether any of them offended against overseas Chinese and occupied their homes. First, we must reach clarity through our investigations. Anyone who has occupied the home of an overseas Chinese must get out. If there is resistance, report it to the provincial party committee. If the resistance continues and the occupying party does not move out, I will invite the indignation of the entire nation by publishing that in *Fujian Daily* and *People's Daily*. We will see who prevails!"

With Xiang Nan paying close personnel attention to the problem, a number of cases that had festered for years involving the seized properties of overseas Chinese were finally resolved. A number of administrative organs or work units were occupying overseas Chinese buildings. Xiang Nan personally oversaw their prompt removal.

Xiang Nan showed extreme courage and sympathy in handling the rehabilitation of a great many cases of false accusations that persisted from past to present. He paid special attention to particularly influential figures from the past and to the problems bequeathed to the present by history.

Aw Boon Haw (known as Hu Wenhu on the mainland), whose ancestral home was located in Fujian's Yongding county, was one of the most famous Chinese business figures in southeast Asia in the 1920s and 1930s. He was called the 'Tiger Balm King'. His products brought benefits to vast numbers of people. After the September 18 incident in 1931, when Japan seized the northeastern provinces, Aw took the lead overseas in raising funds to support resistance against Japan; he made great contributions. But when Japan occupied Hong Kong, Hu emerged as the chairman of the Overseas Chinese Association, and went to Japan. For that reason, after the war was over, he was an object of controversy.

After the establishment of the PRC, Aw Boon Haw on three occasions sent messages to the military administrative commission in the leadership compound of Zhongnanhai, expressing his sincere loyalty to the people's government, but this did not gain fair treatment for Aw and his family. After Xiang Nan came to head the government in Fujian, he received request after request from Aw Boon Haw, asking him to pay serious attention to the policy problems he faced. How to deal with Aw Boon Haw became an important symbol of the principle 'seek truth from facts' and a symbol of whether Fujian would seriously address the policy issues raised by the case.

On 8 April 1983, Xiang Nan and two members of the standing committee of the provincial party committee went to Aw Boon Haw's ancestral town of Xiayang, in Yongding, and publicly announced to the world: "Mr Aw Boon Haw's family had done good things for his native place, and the people of his ancestral home remember him with respect. All of us remember him with respect." Although these words were but a small gesture, their sound quickly reverberated around the entire world. The news and photographs of Xiang Nan's visit to Aw Boon Haw's ancestral home in the rain were promptly reported in the major Hong Kong newspapers, and performed a very good publicity function.

On 20 May 1983, the Fujian provincial government officially approved a report by the cities of Fuzhou and Xiamen recommending the return to Aw Boon Haw of his property and other assets in Fuzhou and Xiamen. A few days later, official announcement of the restoration of these properties took the form of a reply by the governor of the province to a reporter's question. The reply, personally reviewed and edited by Xiang Nan, read as follows: "All property and financial assets of Aw Boon Haw in Fujian are returned to him. We welcome Mr Aw and his descendants, at a time of mutual convenience, to find time to come, or to send representatives to come back and formally receive these assets, according to proper procedures. The provincial government will also release funds to establish the Tiger and Leopard Villa in the Hu clan's ancestral home of Yongding."

Soon after, Guangdong also decided to return to Aw Boon Haw his properties in that province.

Addressing the policy issues in the case of Aw Boon Haw was deeply moving to Aw's eldest daughter, Hu Xian.

At the end of 1992, Hu Xian brought her mother, Hu Chen Jinzhi, on her first visit to Beijing, where they were warmly received by General Secretary Jiang Zemin and Vice-Premier Li Peng. Xiang Nan held a banquet in their honour in the Fujian room of the Great Hall of the People. For Hu Xian, setting foot on one's ancestral soil was the fulfilment of a dream. This event also lent the hope of seeing their own plots of native soil to many other Chinese people in other countries.

Xiang Nan warmly receives Dr Hu Xian, who returned to her family's ancestral location of Yongding, 1994

Chapter 33

Resolutely Combating Smuggling and Trafficking in Smuggled Goods

As China implemented the reform and opening-up policy, its gates to the world opened step by step and the flow of people into China and from China to other countries increased daily. With that came a host of problems that had not arisen in the past. In the early 1980s, as economic development proceeded in a number of places in Guangdong and Fujian provinces, very serious economic criminal activities erupted, including smuggling, trade in smuggled goods and bribery of corrupt officials. In the face of all this, some people viewed the newly-initiated reform and opening-up policy with suspicion.

Xiang Nan was alarmed by the smuggling and trade in smuggled goods appearing along the Fujian coast.

As early as the spring and summer of 1981, Fujian convened two anti-smuggling conferences and resolved to attack smuggling and speculation vigorously and rapidly. In order to strengthen its leadership, the authorities at the provincial level and in key counties, following Xiang Nan's instructions, set up a maritime anti-smuggling force. But Xiang Nan firmly opposed the line of argument that said that 'these capitalist evils have been brought in by the policies of opening up'. He argued that, in the early 1950s, although there was no opening to the outside world, there had nonetheless been plenty of embezzlement and bribery. As he saw it, all economic criminal activity had to be combated, and could be prevented, and should not in any event have any influence on the overall picture of opening up.

On 14 December 1981, Deng Xiaoping put forth a document that had been approved by the central discipline commission (CDC) entitled *Some*

Comrades in Various Work Units in Guangdong and Fujian are Continuing to Engage in Smuggling and Trafficking in Smuggled Goods. He wrote: "The reasons that this kind of activity has not been thoroughly dealt with require careful examination. I recommend that a special small group under the CDC carry out the most thorough investigation. The higher the individual, the bigger the organisation, the more severely this must be dealt with."

In January 1982, in a CDC internal document entitled *Rampant Smuggling at Various Locations in Guangdong*, Chen Yun wrote: "My recommendation is that we punish some severely, kill some, imprison some and publicise all of this in the newspapers. If we don't do that, the party's work style cannot be set right." Following that, the party's central secretariat took up this question, and issued an urgent notice dealing with the attack on smuggling, trafficking and speculation.

On the day that the central secretariat's notice arrived, Xiang Nan passed it out at a conference of local party secretaries, and demanded that all present take this up as a major matter when they returned to their home areas. The standing committee of the provincial party committee carried out its own special investigation, and came out with six principal measures.

On 15 January 1982, Peng Chong, a member of the politburo of the CPC central committee specially sent to Fujian, speaking to a meeting of party organisation department secretaries from all the agencies operating directly under the provincial government, distributed the instruction from the central party standing committee, along with the urgent notice and the central secretariat's opinion on thorough implementation. Peng Chong further offered several additional opinions. That very day, led by Xiang Nan, the standing committee of the Fujian provincial party specially took a number of measures.

Xiang Nan made clear his determination to carry out the instructions from the centre. He remarked: "Smuggling and trafficking in smuggled goods in society is not to be feared; it is the corrosion of our military ranks and our cadres that should cause alarm. Our opposition to smuggling and bribery is set in stone. Our policy of opening up is equally set in stone. We shall not allow the former ills to undermine the latter policy. Just as comrade Peng Chong has said, in implementing the special policies and flexible measures that have been granted to it, Fujian fundamentally still has not taken giant strides forward. This work has still not been made a top priority, and it is extremely insufficient. In seeking to destroy smuggling and trafficking, the centre is not saying that it wants to discard the special policies and flexible measures granted to us; it is not saying that it does not want to proceed with SEZs, or that it doesn't want to carry out opening up."

Xiang Nan continued emphatically: "We must not shrink back in caution because of this and be fearful of doing our work. If our work exposes some ills or we lack experience in dealing with them, all that is understandable. But corruption and bribery for self-enrichment without regard for the nation's interest is inexcusable, and it must be attacked resolutely."

Only 20-odd days later, the party's central secretariat called a special discussion meeting with the full standing committees of the provincial party committees of Guangdong and Fujian. The central matter on the table was how best to act with maximum determination and effectiveness in response to the centre's urgent notice; what next steps to take in expanding the struggle against criminal activities in the economic arena; how to rectify the guiding ideas behind this effort; and how better to carry out the special policies and flexible measures, in order to develop the economies of the two provinces.

After the meeting, Xiang Nan immediately sent out a message expressing the spirit of the meeting and conveying his instructions on powerful new measures to be deployed. In keeping with the centre's urgent messages regarding the 'Two Necessaries' and the 'Two Prohibited Things', the crimes of large-scale plundering of state and collective assets for private gain and similar criminal activities were to be punished with great speed and force. Cadres, especially those in leadership roles, who engaged in such activities were to be punished according to law. The top priority was to deal with responsible cadres under whom such economic problems remained persistent, and to attack major and important cases in which cleanup efforts were dragging on ineffectually. There was to be no relaxation in grasping these challenges, and dealing with them would require firm resolve. Powerful and speedy assaults were necessary. As for coastal areas where smuggling was particularly serious, strong work teams would be dispatched to help in the effort to destroy the smuggling evil.

Chapter 34

'Fujian's Economy Relies on TVEs as the Spearhead'

In 1982, the entire nation opened the 'two strikes' struggle against smuggling, trafficking in smuggled goods and speculation. In Fujian, two small cities – Jinjiang and Shishi – were listed as key target areas.

In the period when the 'two strikes' struggle was emerging, Xiang Nan stated that, as smuggling and trafficking were being attacked on the one

As early as 1982, Xiang Nan advocated a line of thinking that included developing the economy through reform and opening up and promoting the development of a new socialist countryside. Here, in a visit to southern Fujian, he writes an inscription for the building of Fujian's new countryside

hand, it was necessary to strengthen guidance on the other. "We must draw together all the special features of each place, developing their strengths and advantages. Our province boasts many overseas Chinese, we are well informed, we have abundant labour and we're not poor in investment capital. Can we use all these advantages to build up our processing industries using important materials, to put our labour force to work on imported designs, to assemble important components or conduct compensation trade?"

The Fujian provincial party committee and provincial government issued a guidance document that severely attacked smuggling and trafficking, while also permitting the large-scale expansion of processing industries using imported materials. The township of Chendai, in the Jinjiang municipal district, started off by making shoes. Shishi began with piece goods, clothing and food products. Both places quickly began to develop. Soon, visiting business people from the entire nation converged on Jinjiang and Shishi.

With the rapid development of production in Jinjiang and Shishi, smuggling and trafficking decreased. The populace began to feel secure going about their productive activities, and their energies were activated. More than a few began to look at returning to the countryside to invest in and run factories of their own.

In 1982, the inhabitants of the Chendai commune came up with Rmb10m to invest in more than 300 factories of all types. Even Xiang Nan had not imagined that so many enterprises could be funded by households combining their resources. He was amazed and delighted to see, as each village caught on to the situation, how many manufacturing enterprises could be created and how valuable their production could become.

The significance of the Chendai model resided in the fact that, with no government investment at all, the potential resources found among the people themselves had been converted into productive power, and that by making use of overseas capital, technology and telecommunications, it was possible to broaden the development of the rural communities' production of economic goods. But some people said that the only way to be 'socialist' was to have investment by the collective and to have unitary management of all enterprises. Dispersed management of the enterprises was 'capitalist', they alleged, even to the point that Chendai's actions amount to 'capitalist restoration'.

Xiang Nan: Champion of Reform in Fujian

A storm erupted in Fujian and elsewhere over whether this new form of economic activity was 'socialism' or 'capitalism'.

In May 1983, Xiang Nan conducted a further investigation and decided to throw his support behind the new phenomenon of the masses combining their own household resources to invest in enterprises. He brought a large assemblage of 200-300 leading figures from the provincial party committee, agencies directly under the provincial government, and the relevant leading figures from cities and counties to Chendai, and convened a field conference of the entire province's commune and production brigade enterprises.

At the meeting, Xiang Nan explained the experiences of the commune and production brigade enterprises in Chendai, applying the terms 'the three transformations' (specialisation, commercialisation of products, diversification) and 'the three natures' (mass nature, appropriate nature, competitive nature), and made clear that the Chendai commune and production brigade enterprises were 'socialist', and not 'capitalist'.

Xiang Nan also made his attitude clear with respect to the diversity of elements making up the economy of Fujian. In his view, the province faced heavy economic development responsibilities because it was situated on the very front line of the nation's maritime defence. The situation on both sides of the Taiwan Strait was shifting, and reform and opening itself was changing. Only by creating commune and production brigade enterprises (that is, township and village enterprises or TVEs), and attracting investment from Taiwanese and overseas Chinese firms, could Fujian's economy develop rapidly. With his own courage and insight, he affirmed the nature of the commune and production brigade enterprises and warmly proclaimed: "Chendai's commune and brigade enterprises are Fujian's blossoms. I hope that everyone will care for and protect these blossoms, so that flowers like this can bloom throughout our province."

In his speech, Xiang Nan also affirmed his support of other communes, including the Cizao commune in Jinjiang, the Yingqian commune in Changle, the Shijing commune in Nan'an and the Nanyu commune in Minhou, and stated his hopes that the blossoms of the TVEs would flourish and remain beautiful forever.

In addition, Xiang Nan made a promise to the leaders in Chendai: "When the value of your production reaches Rmb100m, I will send you a congratulatory silken banner."

In mid-August, the Fujian province conference of TVEs opened at Jinfeng, in Changle county. In keeping with Fujian's economic situation and the rapid development of TVEs, Xiang Nan sounded a new slogan in a resonant voice: "Fujian's economy relies on TVEs to be the spearhead."

With Xiang Nan's encouragement and guidance, the people of Chendai took advantage of their situation and rose, fully living up to the people's expectations. The value of the township's combined industrial and agricultural production in 1984 surpassed Rmb100m, making Chendai the first 'Rmb100m township' in Fujian. Towards the end of that year, the local party committee and administrative offices again held an awards session. Xiang Nan specially dispatched a member of the provincial party committee to offer congratulations and send a silk banner inscribed with the words: "The flower of township and village enterprise".

Beginning as a typical poor and backward commune, Chendai's transformation into 'Fujian's first Rmb100m township' renowned far and wide, was entirely the result of Xiang Nan's motivation and support. The new rural economic form created by the masses' collection of their own investment capital and management of their own enterprises came to be

Xiang Nan (second from right), with vice-premier and member of the central party secretariat Wan Li (third from right), visit TVEs in Chendai, Jinjiang county, 1984

called by economists the 'Jinjiang model'. This model little resembled the system in southern Jiangsu, where townships and villages collectively managed their enterprises, and it was not similar to the model in southern Zhejiang, where the individual household was the organisational unit. Instead, the Jinjiang model lay between these other two, with anywhere from a few to a dozen or more households jointly managing individual enterprises.

By the time the Chendai field meeting concluded, the single flowering branch of TVEs had already been transformed into 'a hundred flowers blooming and contending'. After a year's development, by 1984, the total value of production by enterprises in Fujian's townships and villages reached Rmb10m, while the number of townships engaged in this manner had risen from 21 to more than 70. Various data show that TVEs had already become the fastest-developing element in the provincial economy, with the greatest vitality and the broadest future ahead of them.

Chapter 35

'The Classic of Mountains and Sea' at the Frontier Extends Its Influence Across the Nation

In putting the agricultural production responsibility system into operation, Xiang Nan started from the particular circumstances of Fujian province. He concluded that the province possessed four great advantages: mountains, oceans, overseas Chinese and 'special policies'. Facing both mountains and the ocean, the province had more than 6.67m hectares in mountainous areas, and tens of thousands of hectares of shallow coastal waters and

Xiang Nan (far right) and Xi Zhongxun, member of the CPC central committee politburo and secretary of the central party secretariat (second from right), visit a rural produce market in Hejiang, located within Fuzhou municipality, February 1983

Xiang Nan (third from right) and Xi Zhongxun (second from right) visit Wuyi mountain, February 1983

mudflats that could be well utilised in development. Moreover, situated in the Asian tropical belt, with a warm climate and plenty of rainfall, the province was a natural greenhouse.

Xiang Nan believed in building upon strengths and minimising weaknesses, giving full rein to one's own advantages. He thought a great deal about the *Classic of Mountains and Seas*, and about constructing Fujian's economy around its eight strengths: forestry, animal husbandry, fishing, economic crops, foreign economic relations, light industry, science and technology, and its potential role in cross-strait unification. This line of thinking found support at all levels throughout the province.

On his first visit to southern Fujian, Xiang Nan observed the slogan 'Take grain as the key link' written on a wall in a coastal county. In his heart, Xiang Nan knew that things were not really like that. Fujian's poverty was itself rooted in 'Taking grain as the key link'. Fujian was short of food grains, including food grains for the military. At the most local level, 99% of party secretaries focused their energies on agriculture; they were known as the 'chemical fertiliser secretaries' or the 'close planting secretaries'. If this situation remained unchanged, when would the economy ever take off?

Not long after Xiang's visit to southern Fujian, the renowned international affairs specialist from the state council's International Problems Research Institute, Huan Xiang, came to Fujian to make a report. He said that South Korea had industrialised in three years, casting agriculture aside while industry prospered. Then, industry was used to support agriculture. As he spoke, some in the audience were denouncing him for "talking nonsense". But 'in line with the adage that great figures think alike', Xiang Nan said that Huan Xiang was right.

When Xiang Nan was supporting the masses' pooling of their resources to invest in manufacturing enterprises, he was becoming increasingly sure that the entire structure of production had to be reordered. That was particularly true of the rural sector's internal structure, which was just starting to encourage development through the growth of TVEs. That meant throwing off the shackles of grain production and tossing Fujian's 'grain-deficient province' label into the Pacific Ocean. The provincial party committee, hearing Xiang's ideas, responded coolly and querulously. 'Tossing the grain-deficient province label into the Pacific Ocean' sounded fine, but what about tax revenue? Would the masses have food? What to do if per capita grain rations were insufficient?

Xiang Nan and Wen Fushan visit a state farm in the outer reaches of Fuzhou

"If grain rations are too low, we can purchase grain from neighbouring provinces or from other countries. Localities and counties can form grain trading companies, make contracts with northern Fujian, and make a good living in the grain trade. In that way, the limited arable land can be put to growing other economic crops including sugar cane, fruit and vegetables. Then, shipping fresh vegetables to the north, the south can bring back corn and sorghum. Bananas and lychees can be exported. Apples and pears can be imported. With this kind of business up and running, commerce can promote the larger development of the economy.

"For Fujian's rural economy to grow by several multiples, we must resolve to change the internal structures of agriculture, abandoning 'Take grain as the key link', freeing ourselves of the burden of 'self-sufficiency in food grain', and turning ourselves to diversified operations. In short, we must plant what is most suitable for the soil and take the route of intensive agriculture."

Xiang Nan thus cast aside the slogan 'Take grain as the key link', strongly promoted the *Classic of Mountains and Seas*, and encouraged rural dwellers to employ diversified operations in accordance with specific local conditions. Throughout the province, everyone rushed to follow the *Classic of Mountains and Seas* according to local realities, busily taking inspiration from the text, rationally opening the resources of mountains and seas for development, and energetically developing the 'mountains and seas' economy. In typical counties and townships, groups of specialised households or specialised villages sprang up, and soon the 'king of wood-ear fungus', the 'king of fragrant mushrooms' and the 'king of sugarcane' were famous nationwide.

On the basis of paying close attention to the *Classic of Mountains and Seas* slogan, what began in the frontier province of Fujian had a clear influence on the entire country.

Chapter 36

Deng Xiaoping Inspects Xiamen SEZ, and Xiang Nan Bravely Speaks Up

On his first visit to Xiamen SEZ, Xiang Nan knitted his brows.

At that time, the SEZ was confined to Huli, with an area of 2.5 square kilometres on Xiamen island. What could be done with such a pint-sized plot of land?

When Vice-Premier Gu Mu visited the SEZ, Xiang Nan told him that an SEZ with only 2.5 square kilometres could never succeed, and that the zone should be enlarged to encompass the entire island. Gu Mu fully agreed with Xiang's view, but, while it was easy to talk about expanding the zone, it had to be approved by the party centre.

Xiang Nan introduces the idea of expanding Xiamen SEZ to encompass all of Xiamen island to Deng Xiaoping, while on a boat tour around Gulangyu

Xiang Nan immediately set to work on the project of expanding Xiamen SEZ to cover all of Xiamen island. He was also hoping that the centre would grant a series of special policies to Fuzhou, the best of them being permission to set up a similar SEZ there. When the general secretary of the party, Hu Yaobang, visited Fujian in 1982, Xiang Nan raised the grand idea of expanding Xiamen SEZ and won Hu's confirmation.

But around that time, the SEZ ran into a period of unprecedented economic cooling, and the battle over whether SEZs were 'socialist' or 'capitalist' was again raging noisily.

In September 1983, at a Fujian SEZ work conference, Xiang Nan proposed that SEZs realise the 'four specials' – special missions, special policies, special environments and special methodologies. Once this speech, entitled 'SEZs Need the Four Specials', was published in the *China SEZ Yearbook* in Hong Kong, it was reprinted in the *Hong Kong Economic News*, the Japanese publication *Chinese Economic Trends* and other publications. Thus Xiang Nan expressed his views on SEZ development and his determination to advance Xiamen SEZ, both domestically and abroad.

Xiang Nan accompanies Deng Xiaoping on an inspection of the docks in Dongdu harbour, 1984

In late January 1984, Deng Xiaoping made an inspection visit to the Shenzhen and Zhuhai SEZs. In early February, he arrived in Xiamen. On 7 February, Xiang Nan presented his report on the establishment of Xiamen SEZ to Deng and Wang Zhen. Deng nodded his approval to Xiang's decision to proceed with basic infrastructure work, remarking: "That is the right way to go about this. If we plant beautiful trees, we will attract beautiful birds. We have to reform and improve our investment environment."

Deng also said: "The best way to proceed is to recruit foreign investment to participate in the construction of the foundations."

After breakfast on 8 February, Deng Xiaoping, the promoter of China's SEZs, came to visit the port of Dongdu, and took a look at construction work on several docks capable of handling 10,000-ton ships. At a dock in Xiamen, he boarded a tour boat named the Lujiang (Heron River).

The tour boat cruised slowly around Gulangyu. Once Xiang Nan had taken his seat next to Deng Xiaoping, he opened a large map of Xiamen that he had specially prepared. Although, under Xiang Nan's encouragement, the special zone was still confined to 2.5 square kilometres, factories outside the zone were receiving the same treatment as enterprises within it.

Xiang Nan accompanies Deng Xiaoping on a visit to the village of Jimeixue

Xiang Nan: Champion of Reform in Fujian

But, at the end of the day, this was illegal, and foreigners, who assumed that the SEZ was only the size of the palm of the hand, were not enthusiastic about investing and building enterprises.

Xiang's report to Deng opened the door to a larger vision. "Comrade Xiaoping, today Xiamen SEZ is only 2.5 square kilometres in area. It is simply too small and restricted. Even if it is completely built out, it will be of little actual significance."

Deng asked: "What is your concrete thinking on this?"

Xiang replied: "The best thing to do is expand the zone to cover the entire island. If we make all of Xiamen island into an SEZ, we can do a much better job at introducing foreign capital and technology, modernising the older enterprises already on the island and firming up cross-strait contacts."

Deng listened to Xiang's report and peered at his map. After a moment's thought, he said in a decisive tone: "I say it can be done."

After a little while, Deng Xiaoping said to Xiang Nan: "After the SEZ is expanded, what is your thinking on how to operate it?"

That question, inseparable from the question of establishing a free port, was the second matter that Xiang Nan wanted to discuss with Deng.

Xiang Nan chats with Deng Xiaoping and Wang Zhen at the Huangyan tower, on Gulangyu

Deng Xiaoping Inspects Xiamen SEZ, and Xiang Nan Bravely Speaks Up

Xiang Nan (front row, left) and Deng Xiaoping plant commemorative trees in Xiamen's Wanshishan botanical park, February 1984

In July 1981, the Fujian party committee received a document entitled *Opinions on the Development of Xiamen SEZ* from the overseas Chinese figure Li Yintong, who lived in Thailand and whose ancestral home was in Fujian. In Li's view, Xiamen SEZ was too small and could not be compared to Shenzhen or Zhuhai, whose proximity to Hong Kong and Macau enabled them to make use of those free ports. For those reasons, Xiamen SEZ needed to be enlarged. Li proposed the establishment of a free port in Xiamen. Xiang Nan had long understood the idea of a free port, and was eager to see Xiamen SEZ expanded. He paid great attention to the document he received from Li Yintong, and ordered the party secretary of Xiamen city, Lu Zifen, to accompany Li Yintong to the province in order to explain the free port idea to the provincial party standing committee.

Xiang Nan had already broached the idea of a Xiamen free port with a number of visiting dignitaries, but the idea was too sophisticated, and he had not received much in the way of response.

Xiang Nan was persistent, and decided to raise the idea again while Deng Xiaoping was inspecting Xiamen. He said to Deng, by way of introduction: "These days, many of our fellow Chinese from Taiwan as well as overseas Chinese are coming to the mainland, but they can't come and go directly. Instead, they have to travel via Hong Kong or Japan, which really is too much bother. If we could build a free port in Xiamen, our closest point to the Jinmen islands and Taiwan, the facilitation of freer travel, the enhancement of ties between people on both sides of the Taiwan Strait, and the promotion of incoming foreign investment can all play big promotional roles."

Deng Xiaoping clearly found this idea very interesting. Xiang Nan had some of the leading officials of Xiamen municipality provide Deng with various materials dealing with free ports, and make their own reports directly to Deng on concrete aspects of developing a Xiamen free port.

Xiang Nan said to Deng Xiaoping, if Hong Kong's approach is examined, there are three issues to consider with respect to free ports. Number one is the free movement of cargoes in and out. Number two is the free passage of people, both in and out. And number three is the free conversion of currencies.

Xiang Nan with Deng Xiaoping and Wang Zhen inspect a military unit in Minhai

Deng replied: "The first two are fine. But how are you going to convert people's money?"

Xiang Nan answered: "I think we could print 'SEZ currency'."

Deng Xiaoping said nothing, and was lost in thought.

Xiang Nan saw that Deng was leaving the door ajar, and that he was thinking excitedly, so he went further: "Without developing Xiamen SEZ, we will still not be able to meet the challenge of transforming Fujian from poverty to wealth. Best of all would be to open up the entire triangle of Xiamen, Zhangzhou and Quanzhou."

Deng responded: "On that, you'll have to wait until I return to Beijing and examine it with the comrades on full-time active duty."

On 9 February, after Xiang Nan accompanied Deng Xiaoping on a tour of Huli industrial district, he happily put pen to paper with the inscription "Operate the SEZ even more rapidly and even better".

Leaving Huli, Xiang Nan and Deng paid a visit to Xiamen international airport. On the previous day, on the ride from Riguangyan to the tour boat dock along a tree-lined road, Xiang Nan had filled Deng in on the international airport.

Xiang Nan (far right) visits the renowned author Ding Ling (second from right) and the famous mathematician Cheng Jingrun (second from left) while they were recovering their health on Gulangyu, 1984

Seeing is believing. Xiamen international airport was rapidly coming into existence. Wang Zhen said over and over again: "Well done! Well done!" Deng Xiaoping's face broke into a smile as he asked Xiang Nan: "Why do you call this an international airport?"

Xiang Nan responded: "If you build an SEZ, you have to build the broadest contact with the outside, and that means an international airport. It is good for reform and opening up. But it is not only for letting people fly in; it also allows people to fly out. And it is not only good for building contact with southeast Asia; we want flights from Japan and the US, too. In the future, we will be able to fly to Taiwan, to the US. Opening up even more widely will require that we are able to fly out to the world."

Deng Xiaoping replied loudly: "Flying out is fine. We really must do more flying out!"

Xiamen international airport did not disappoint expectations, and today it is known far and wide as an airport of the first rank.

Deng Xiaoping's visit to Xiamen SEZ unquestionably gave a huge boost to the zone's development.

Xiang Nan (third from right) and Wan Li (fourth from right) view a model of SEZ construction while inspecting Xiamen SEZ, January 1985

Xiang Nan (right) accompanies Deng Yingchao, chair of the CPPCC (third from right) on a visit to Xiamen SEZ

On 18 March 1984, Hu Yaobang met with a delegation from the alliance of China-Japan friendly legislators led by the Japanese friendly figure Ito Masayoshi. Hu Yaobang said to the Japanese guests: "China's implementation of the policy of opening up is not a matter of closing up but rather a matter of continued opening. This has emerged from Deng Xiaoping's February trip to the Shenzhen and Xiamen SEZs. We comrades in the central leadership have strongly approved his recommendations."

Hu Yaobang said: "We have now decided to expand Xiamen SEZ from its original 2.5 square kilometre area to encompass the entire island of Xiamen. Moreover, along our coastline, we have selected a series of cities, from Dalian in Liaoning province in the north to Beihai in Guangxi in the south, for the application of a series of special policies. In this manner, we seek to welcome foreign friends to build joint venture enterprises or wholly-owned foreign enterprises, including wholly-owned hotels."

On 29 June 1985, the state council issued its official reply to the Fujian provincial government's *Report on Matters Relating to the Implementation*

Xiang Nan (left) with Fujian Provincial Governor Jia Qinglin (centre) inspect construction work in the Xiamen port district, 1991

of the Programme for Xiamen SEZ, and authorised the expansion of the SEZ to include the entire island of Xiamen as well as Gulangyu. The state council further approved the step-by-step implementation of policies related to the development of a free port. When this *Document 85* appeared, Xiamen responded by building an SEZ that kept industry as the core but also included tourism, commerce and real estate in a comprehensive, outward-facing special zone.

Thus the partial blueprint for Xiamen SEZ that Xiang Nan had sketched was finally realised, and the zone moved into a new phase of comparatively rapid development.

Chapter 37

Breaking Through Layers of Obstruction to Recruit Foreign-Invested Projects

On more than one occasion, under a variety of circumstances, Xiang Nan made the point that after China's long period of self-imposed isolation, building economic development was slow, while the weak industrial foundation was detrimental to modernising construction. If industry was to advance, then it was essential to set about the task of introducing elements from outside China and relaxing the grip of the state so that enterprises could go about getting their jobs done.

Xiang Nan was extremely active on matters relating to foreign inputs, even to the point of participating personally in some negotiations. He said: "We absolutely must open our gates wide and fiercely set about importing foreign inputs. If there are deals to be closed, they should be closed on the spot, without a lot of dithering. We must not bungle our opportunities by imposing layer after layer of approvals. In short, and in keeping with the state council leadership's spirit of 'passing approval powers down one level' somewhat, we must relax our hold and get things done."

In the old Yongding district of western Fujian, a patriotic overseas Chinese figure wanted to do everything he could for the development of his old homeland. He started a wholly-owned rattan ware venture, brought in imported rattan and recruited unemployed young people living at home to take up weaving the material. Then he exported his products to foreign markets. Thanks to Xiang Nan's comments, the county authorities approved the project, as did the local party committee. But when all this was sent up to the provincial level, the only response was silence. The county authorities asked the district, and the district officials wrote to Xiang Nan to find out why the province was not approving the project. Xiang Nan approached the responsible figure in the provincial economic commission, who said:

"We're not the ones who haven't approved this; it is the state economic commission that won't do so. They have not issued the licence, and this rattan may not be imported."

Things like this still occurring! Why was something as fine as this not approved? Xiang Nan gave a call to an old and close friend, Vice-Minister Wei Yuming of the ministry of foreign economic relations and trade (Mofert). "Why does a project like this need approval from your ministry? Are you out to kill this project?"

Wei Yuming replied: "There's no need for any approval."

"All right, then, I am going to tell the county to let them import the goods."

"Fine," Wei Yuming said with certainty.

But Xiang Nan didn't imagine that, the very next day, the provincial authorities would receive a message from Mofert, stating that permission was not granted. On hearing this, Xiang Nan was furious. When next in Beijing for the NPC, he made a special visit to the central party secretariat to tell them how things stood with Mofert. Hu Yaobang wrote to Minister Chen Muhua, who replied to Hu. In her report to Hu, Chen wrote: "The denial of approval for Fujian in this case is entirely justified. First, there are already a great many rattan factories in China, their sales channels are problematic and adding to production will simply make the pressures worse. Second, importing rattan will require foreign exchange. Third, they have no advanced technology in the project. So our ministry has considered all this and denied approval."

In passing this message on to Xiang Nan, Hu Yaobang marked it with a circle to indicate he had read it, but neither disagreed nor agreed with its content.

The problem was unresolved, and Xiang Nan was at a loss. He could not help getting very angry. "This is a wholly-owned foreign invested enterprise, not a Sino-foreign joint venture. What actions of his do you think you control?" If clearly beneficial projects like this all run into such interference, there will be absolutely no modern technology. What hope will we have for our country's opening up?"

Seeing that Xiang Nan was implacable, the ministry came up with a compromise proposal. To Fujian it said: "We agree on this particular project. But Xiang Nan is still brooding about this. He is not doing this for himself – he is instead thinking about our national image. The image of one single open province can have negative effects on the way the overseas Chinese view the entire nation. Taking a matter as small as this to the general secretary, and we even hear it has been sent to Chen Yun; the noisier this gets, the more complex it becomes."

After reading Xiang Nan's report, Chen Yun said: "Comrade Xiang Nan's opinion is correct." It was only under these circumstances that the ministry finally agreed.

In August 1984, the establishment of the first foreign-invested enterprise in western Fujian – Yongqiao Rattan Enterprise – was formally signed. Modern equipment was imported from the firm Xinyihang in Hong Kong, and the funds from the sole investor went to running a business dealing in various rattan raw materials as well as rattan furniture and rattan handicraft products. All production was sold abroad. The matter was successfully concluded, but only those directly connected with it got a taste of what lessons could be learned.

This experience led Xiang Nan to believe that this kind of multi-level application-and-approval process, to say nothing of the stifling effects of endless office-by-office procedural blockages, could not go on. Powers of authorisation would have to be loosened, from the central authorities above, down through the provincial level to the localities and municipalities. The centre would have to release powers to the localities. The province would have to release many kinds of authority to the localities at the municipal and county levels. Xiang Nan said publicly: "In opening up as far as we have, we haven't experienced a single instance of disorder resulting from the downward devolution of authority. Instead, what Fujian has often witnessed have been dysfunctions arising from the failure to release such authority downward. But failing to assign such powers to lower levels can produce confusion; if such authority does migrate downward, there may be no confusion at all; at worst, any confusion that does arise will be small-scale."

The more selfless, the more fearless. In late 1984, while at a national conference on guidance planning, Xiang Nan picked up the old themes with a number of leading comrades, saying to them with great feeling: "On this one little project, I encountered so many difficulties. The application and approval process took two years. If the province was completely unable to approve a project like this, how can we open up the whole process of working on foreign economic matters? Needless to say, central agencies should not be concerning themselves with projects like these. Even at the provincial level, there are too many of these projects to control. Most should be handled at the county level – that would be enough. As for slightly larger projects, procedures take even longer. Some projects go through three years of discussion with no decisions. Some overseas Chinese come to see that this is a marathon, to see who can outlast whom. How can we 'open up' with situations like this? How can we carry through on comrade Deng Xiaoping's strategy of openness to the outside?"

Xiang Nan added: "The 'relaxation' we advocate so strongly includes not only the emancipation of thinking and the downward devolution of administrative powers; policies and plans must be relaxed at the same time. The economy of Fujian must grow. Asking the centre to give us such-and-such investments, and asking them to arrange such-and-such projects for us, is out of touch with reality today. All we ask is that the centre provides the policy framework and hands over various authorities to the provinces, with some of those powers going further down to the cities and counties."

Xiang Nan stated frankly that he himself had been full of enthusiasm originally when he met with foreign business people, and of hopes for many projects that would propel Fujian's economy forward. But after a while, he came to feel how difficult it all was. In discussions with foreign business people, he understood that he had to provide solid, thorough responses: "Yes. We can do it." But experience proved that this was not so simple. After a number of bitter lessons, Xiang Nan was unable to offer any certain answers. He said: "I have said 'We can do it' countless times. But if I say 'We can accomplish this', what am I to do if the higher levels don't approve?

"It is not only industry that needs to import. Agriculture needs to as well, whether it be modern technology or superior seed strains or breeding stock. All of that is ultimately for the final purpose of going out into the world." That was Xiang Nan's distinctive perspective. He ran meetings of the standing committee of the provincial party committee many, many times, elaborating on the subject of agricultural imports. Under his leadership, over a long period of time, Fujian came to lead the nation in agricultural projects involving importation of advanced inputs.

Chapter 38

Deciding the Fate of Enterprises by Loosening Administrative Approval Processes

Once Xiang Nan assumed political leadership in Fujian, reform of the rural economy made increasingly rapid progress, thanks to the central role assigned to the household contract responsibility system. After two years, production in the rural sector was showing excellent results. But by 1983, the economic performance of Fujian's businesses was far from ideal. Enterprises were hobbled by their own pressures and by the shackles of inherited operational styles that prevented them from rousing themselves. On all sides – production, supply, distribution, personnel, finance, materials

Xiang Nan (second from right, front row) and Wu Hongxiang, chairman of the Fujian CPPCC (front row, right), visit a state-owned enterprise, 1982

— enterprises were bound hand and foot by the pathology of 'unity': unified plans sent down from higher authorities, unified systems of material resource supplies, unified administration of product sales, unified pricing systems, unified personnel arrangements, unified determination of wage levels, unified revenue and expenditure systems, and so on.

On 23 March 1984, a conference of 55 provincial factory chiefs and managers in Fuzhou produced a letter with a heartfelt and bold appeal: "Please loosen our shackles." They sent it to Xiang Nan.

In their letter, they described how the maze of regulations and restrictions tied their hands; enterprises had no powers to act; dreaming of greater vigour was out of the question. The letter asked the provincial party committee and the provincial government to permit enterprises to exercise five different types of authority, including the power to hire and fire their own cadres and to issue bonuses.

Xiang Nan read the message, and quickly issued an instruction. "The tone of this message is sincere. It leaves the reader convinced that we cannot progress if we don't pursue further reform and if we don't further

Xiang Nan joins CPC politburo member and CPC secretariat member Lu Dingyi to inspect Fuzhou, January 1984

relax the restrictions on decision-making powers. I think this letter should be made public for all to read."

The next day, *Fujian Daily* printed the letter from the 55 factory chiefs and managers in full on its front page. Xiang Nan also wrote his own short and intense note of guidance. This quick response to their message, and the high level of attention it gained, went far beyond the expectations of the factory managers.

A single stone can cause huge ripples. Publication of the factory managers' heartfelt cry immediately provoked a chain reaction of responses.

On 30 March, *People's Daily* printed, on the first page of its second section, the 24 March *Fujian Daily's* appeal, and *Fujian Daily's* report of 25 March on the provincial party committee's organisation department's supportive message in response. *People's Daily* editors added: "This letter of appeal raises an important question regarding structural reform." The time had come: failure to eliminate these accumulated blockages inherited from past practice was no longer an option. Other major national media outlets, including *Economic Daily* and China Central Television, added their reprints and rebroadcasts.

On 15 April, the state commission on structural reform and the state economic commission (SEC) invited five representatives of the original 55 factory heads and managers to Beijing to discuss their appeal for 'loosening the shackles' and other questions of economic structural reform.

Xiang Nan returns from the 'two sessions' in Beijing, 1984

Xiang Nan presents a report to the fourth congress of the Communist Party of Fujian, June 1985

Tong Dalin, the renowned economist and deputy chairman of the structural reform commission, held three seminars. He asserted: "'Loosening the shackles' is not only a matter of structural reform; it is like throwing a stone into the pool of our entire economic work."

Yuan Baohua, vice-chairman of the SEC, said to the factory representatives: "You have done something good; the active support shown by the provincial party committee and the provincial government, and the measures they have adopted, have received positive reviews by the relevant central organs and leaders." The five Fujian representatives were invited to visit the central party school, where the party magazine *Red Flag* convened another seminar.

At a time when large-scale reform of the national system of state-owned enterprises had not yet gained traction, and Fujian factory directors and managers had raised their appeal to revitalise their enterprises on five separate fronts, Xiang Nan argued that putting 'relaxation of powers' in the newspapers was not enough: more emphasis needed to be placed on implementation and achieving good results.

Deciding the Fate of Enterprises by Loosening Administrative Approval Processes

At a conference on Fujian's industry and trade on 10 April, Xiang Nan asserted: "If we want to invigorate our enterprises and improve their strengths, the essential problem is one of reform, and the core of reform is the loosening of restrictions on decision-making. We have to ensure that our factory directors and managers retain personnel powers, and financial and operating authority. Without giving them these three forms of authority, to put it bluntly, their enterprises will not be well run. I hope that all government agencies and party committees, all bureau and department heads will act as the provincial party committee and provincial government have: at all times, consider the difficulties facing these directors and managers. Untie the bonds that ensnare them, and let them advance. Let them develop. Let them take flight."

On 24 April, a month after publication of the letter appealing for a 'loosening of the shackles', the standing committee of the Fujian provincial party committee and the party organisation within the provincial government came up with their decision: they called another session with the 55 factory directors and managers for the middle of May to investigate further the question of 'loosening the shackles'. Xiang Nan personally wrote

Xiang Nan casts a vote at the fourth congress of the Communist Party of Fujian, 1985

Xiang Nan with Xi Jinping in Fuzhou, 1994

an article regarding that session, and published it in *Fujian Daily*, under the headline, "The provincial party committee has decided to convene another meeting of the 55 directors and managers in mid-May to proceed with their investigation. What sorts of powers have yet to be taken in hand? What restraints have still not been released?"

He wrote:"Yesterday, the standing committee of the provincial party committee and the provincial government's party organisation, at their meeting on rectifying the party, came out with a decision: they would again convene a meeting with the 55 factory directors and managers, in mid-May, to proceed further with their investigation of the questions relating to 'loosening the shackles': which powers are still not in the managers' hands, and what restraining bonds have still not been released; who is dealing well with the challenge of 'loosening the shackles', who is still clinging to powers that should be delegated downward, and who is not helping at all to 'loosen the shackles'. This meeting is going to name names. It is going to come up with the specific organisational units and individuals who are promoting reform and it is going to come up with the specific units and responsible individuals who are blocking the path of economic reform. It will advance the enlargement of enterprise autonomy and take a step forward towards eliminating enterprises' status as constituent units of government administrative structures."

Xiang Nan's short and pithy message gave strong encouragement to the reformers. To those standing on the sidelines, his message provided direction, but also reminded them that they were subject to supervision.

Xiang Nan with his wife Wang Zhixin in Fuzhou, 1994

In the early period of reform and opening up and the liberation of thinking, Fujian was the first to raise the question of 'loosening the shackles', delegating decision-making powers downward and expanding enterprise autonomy. This was the beginning of national enterprise reform and the ensuing movement to separate government from enterprise.

On 10 May 1984, the state council issued its *Provisional Regulations Regarding the Expansion of Autonomy for State-Owned Enterprises*, thus affirming the devolution of decision-making powers sought by the enterprises. On 12 May, *People's Daily* ran an article under the headline "The response to the appeal for 'loosening the shackles' has drawn open the curtain on reform: let the factory directors, who are committed to reform and brave enough to undertake reforms, return to their plants and show real results." *People's Daily* reported on the situation in Fujian after the 55 directors and managers returned to their factories to carry out reforms, and bestowed high praise on them for their methods.

Seeing that many enterprises still clung to the habit of 'everyone eating from the same big pot', Xiang Nan advocated the elimination of egalitarianism in the assignment of jobs, and called for the energetic elimination of the twin evils of 'enterprises feeding from the nation's big pot' and of enterprise staff and workers 'feeding from the enterprise's big pot'. Xiang Nan demanded that the word 'contract' enter the vocabulary of the enterprises. He called for enterprises to adopt the contract responsibility system, with each team in the enterprise committing to set goals, and responsibility falling onto each individual's shoulders. This, Xiang Nan argued, would finally fully arouse the activism of the enterprises and their workers and staff personnel.

The twin reforms of 'loosening of the shackles', and inserting the key word 'contract' into the common vocabulary, touched on problems at the deepest level of reform. Today, these things seem routine. But in the circumstances of the time, Xiang Nan's daring in supporting them and carrying them out produced ripples in the pond at a thousand levels, and required enormous courage and fortitude.

In February 1994, to commemorate this historic 'loosening of the shackles' and expansion of enterprise autonomy on the 10th anniversary of the policies, the China enterprise management association and the China entrepreneurs association announced a decision: thenceforth, 21 April was designated National Entrepreneurs Day.

Xiang Nan and Wang Zhixin in Fuzhou, 1994

Chapter 39

The Controversy over 'Jinjiang Fake Medicines'

On 16 June 1985, China National Radio made public news of a national conference focused on China's pharmaceutical management, and charging that the area of Jinjiang in Fujian province was producing and selling fake drug products. At the conference, the minister of public health, Cui Yueli, levelled criticisms at the relevant government bodies in Fujian and demanded that the legal system show no leniency in getting to the bottom of the fake drug case. The broadcast added: "All will be waiting to see what will be done with those illegal elements who are making and selling these fake drugs."

The same day, *People's Daily* published an article entitled 'The chilling case of counterfeit drugs in Jinjiang, Fujian province'. Public criticism by *People's Daily* was no trivial affair.

Xiang Nan was in eastern Fujian on an inspection visit when he heard the broadcast. He quickly had his secretary call the provincial party committee and demanded that they call a meeting immediately with cadres from the Jinjiang district and Jinjiang county party committees, to come up with a response to this matter. He demanded an attitude of full recognition, and ordered the full mobilisation of every power to put into effect whatever measures were needed to handle the issue of fake and harmful drugs. When he got back to Fuzhou, he immediately organised a meeting between the relevant provincial agencies and the investigative team sent to Jinjiang from the ministry of public health. Investigation of the counterfeit drug case continued, coordinated by working groups at the local and county level.

The 'Jinjiang counterfeit drugs case' actually began with illegal behaviour by individual rural inhabitants of Hankou village in the county township of Chendai. Chendai township was a place with a high concentration of residents belonging to the Hui minority nationality. In the years when 'taking class struggle as the key link' prevailed, class struggle there was especially severe. Armed conflicts burst out over and over, pitting farmer against farmer and members of a religious ethnic group against one another, and reopening ancient hatreds that had persisted for a hundred years. After the third plenum of the 11th party congress, and particularly after Xiang Nan's speech in support of TVEs, the turbulence among the masses gradually calmed down as people turned their thoughts to developing the economy, the TVEs and the privately-operated economy. But one concomitant of this bounding economy was the negative phenomenon of pursuing profits without regard to anything else. The sale and distribution of counterfeit food products and pharmaceuticals was a typical example.

The investigation revealed that the centre of fake drug manufacturing and sales was the village of Hankou in Chendai township. This village had 2,600 residents, and about 64 hectares of cultivable land. The amount of available land per capita was insufficient by about one twelfth of an acre. Starting in the early 1980s, Hankou turned to producing great quantities of the edible fungus known as 'white wood ear', but the popularisation of improved technologies led to major production increases and the market price for their product dropped steeply. Village cadres and others with a facility for business figured out a way of adding sugar to white wood ear to make and sell a clear beverage. Unable to find sales channels for the product, they then added pharmaceutical-sounding words such as 'medicinal powder' and on the packaging printed explanatory phrases about 'reinforcing the yin' and 'moistening the lungs, best used for controlling fatigue and cough'. They also made contact with pharmaceutical-connected government agencies in Fujian and elsewhere to push their products, offering them sales commissions. An upward flurry of sales ensued, reaching more than Rmb8m. While these beverages actually contained no harmful ingredients, it was obviously a major mistake to claim medicinal properties for them.

The provincial party committee had long been firmly opposed to such improper and possibly illegal tactics. Xiang Nan's attitude was clear and consistent: TVEs needed support and they needed to grow, but illegal activities had to be severely attacked. He said many times: "We have to pay attention to quality if the TVEs are to be able to stand with their feet firmly planted."

In fact, after the 'Jinjiang fake drug case' broke in early 1985, the Fujian provincial party committee and provincial government assigned the highest priority to the problem. Although Xiang Nan had wholeheartedly approved of the rise of TVEs, calling them the "blossoming flower" of Fujian's economic development, he was firmly opposed to what Hankou had done in calling a beverage made from white wood ear fungus a remedy for the common cold. He announced that methods such as this were completely erroneous, and rapidly made an accurate report on the problem to the party centre, assuming leadership of the investigative effort and at the same time taking decisive action by ordering the strictest handling of the affair. What he had not imagined was that newspapers, television stations and radio broadcasters from all over China would descend on Jinjiang, demanding that the Fujian party committee examine its own failings in the case. Figures in the central party leadership issued their own denunciations of the fake pharmaceutical affair.

With the media endlessly repeating the same stories, what had begun as a case of a single village producing fake pharmaceuticals mushroomed quickly. The township and village enterprises in the county of Jinjiang and the entire Jinjiang district, once singled out by Xiang Nan as the "flowering blossom of TVEs", now fell under heavy assault, unable to sell their products, barred from commercial sales shows, while masses of goods withdrawn from sale flowed back, to the point that when Jinjiang natives travelled on business, hotels refused them entry. Over time, many Jinjiang district TVEs, like tiny boats engulfed by wind and storms, stared utter destruction in the face.

At this most difficult of moments, Xiang Nan stood forth. In mid-July, in the township of Jiangkou, in Putian county, Fujian held a TVE field meeting. In his remarks, Xiang Nan offered criticism of a number of problems relating to the fake drugs case. But he also added his words of support and concern for the enterprises that had managed to come such a long way in the face of so many challenges. He denounced the invective hurled at the enterprises of Chendai township and the entire province of Fujian, which had caused them to fall into their present difficulties. Xiang

Nan stated: "This is a case of 10 being blamed for the misdeeds of one. Henceforth, we have to make even greater strides on the road to reform, paying constant attention to plucking out the harmful weeds, and making sure that our TVEs will enjoy their opportunities to prosper."

Xiang Nan's speech was extremely moving to those in Chendai township and among TVE leaders throughout Fujian. With criticism descending on them from the centre, and the entire nation's media casting blame, to hear Xiang Nan's fair remarks was almost too much to bear! Extremely touched, the TVE leaders vowed they would not disappoint Xiang Nan's expectations, and that they would indeed, on the road to reform, pull up the noxious weeds, preserve their chances for prosperity and continue to make great forward strides.

Xiang Nan and the Fujian provincial party committee handled the fake drug case firmly, and the measures they took were strong. They halted the production and sale of the fake drugs, blocked any further inundations, and meted out appropriate punishments to those principally responsible. But who would have imagined that, in coming days, there would be others who would go to extremes to replicate the ferment of the 'Jinjiang fake drugs case'? The influence of that affair lasted for many years after Xiang Nan had departed Fujian.

Shrouded in the shadow of the 'Jinjiang fake drugs case', Xiang Nan had never hesitated nor flinched in doing his job, and never turned away from the tasks to which he had committed himself. His confidence in perpetually pushing for reform and opening up never faltered. He said: "Reform is a kind of revolution; it is certainly true that some people support it and others oppose it. Those who oppose want to excoriate you. We can only stiffen our backs and toughen our skins and let them scold. While they rage for six months or a year, our situation will change, and our economy will become more vibrant, and then they will stop scolding. They might even praise you for your farsightedness."

As a reformer who had seen innumerable political storms over time, Xiang Nan, with his unique vision, said this to one and all: "Over the next several years, it is going to be very hard to think about reform free of difficulties. Taking everything into account in advance would be the thorough thing to do, but if you think you can wait until you have thought of everything before acting on reform, you might as well not bother with reform at all."

At another meeting prior to his departure from Fujian, Xiang Nan expressed his standpoint with clarity. "Reform and opening up represent something new in life. No one can avoid some loss. Reform and opening up indeed present gains and losses. But we may be certain of this: the gains from reform far, far outweigh the losses. And so we can definitely say: our pursuit of reform and opening up is correct, successful and unwavering. If, along the path to reform and opening up, we only look upon the unhealthy things and concentrate on the mistakes, and we waver in our wise decisions or even turn away from them, such an attitude would be extremely mistaken. A Communist Party member must always, under all circumstances, clearly understand the relationship between the main current and the smaller side currents, the relationship between the essential nature of a thing and its surface manifestations."

In late March 1986, Xiang Nan took Chen Guangyi, who had been assigned by the party centre to succeed him, on a tiring journey to the coastal regions and cities of Putian, Zhangzhou, Xiamen and Quanzhou to introduce him to Fujian's situation.

Xiang Nan had not forgotten Chendai township in Jinjiang county, which was still immersed in a storm of controversy. He deliberately

After 30 years of development, Jinjiang in Fujian has become a symbol of China's reform and opening up, and an economic model of a Chinese county capital city

brought Chen Guangyi to Hankou village, whose cadres nervously told the two visiting leaders about conditions there in the aftermath of the Jinjiang fake drugs case. They made clear that they hoped to learn lessons from the case, and in the future to build actively on the advantage that their overseas Chinese contacts offered. They committed to leading their TVEs in the direction of healthy development. When Xiang Nan had first learned about the outcomes of the fake drug case, Rmb130,000 earned by the village's enterprises had been confiscated. Now, Xiang Nan told Chen Guangyi that the money should be given back to the village. As he was about to leave the village, Xiang Nan specially urged the Jinjiang party secretary to return that sum to the villagers.

Chapter 40

With Deep Feeling, Bidding Farewell to Fujian at 67

In 1984, Xiang Nan had recommended to the party centre that a younger comrade succeed him as secretary of the Fujian provincial party committee. Xiang was 65. At that time, 65 was the age limit for officials of provincial and ministerial rank. For the sake of stability, the party centre decided that a number of provincial and autonomous region leaders, including Xiang Nan, should extend their tenures for a brief additional period.

In 1985, the centre arranged for Xiang Nan to serve as the deputy leader of a CPC delegation. Xiang, together with the party politburo member and

Xiang Nan (third from right) with Fang Yi, a member of the party central committee politburo and central secretariat (second from left) on a visit to Nanping, 1985

central secretariat member, Hu Qili, took the delegation on a visit to the Federal Republic of Germany (West Germany).

A meeting of a CPC delegation with the German Democratic Socialist Party. Xiang Nan is far left, next to Hu Qili, while Li Shujing is third from right

Xiang Nan exchanges gifts with the chairman of the German Democratic Socialist Party, Willy Brandt

The CPC delegation visits the research centre on Marxism in the Federal Republic of Germany

The CPC delegation tours the KKG nuclear power plant's information centre in the Federal Republic of Germany

Xiang Nan (fifth from left) with Yang Shangkun (sixth from left) receiving leaders of PLA units stationed in Fujian, February 1986

In May 1985, Xiang Nan attended a session celebrating the inauguration of the Fuzhou-Mawei highway tunnel constructed by military units based in Fuzhou. He points to the lofty and fearless spirit, emphasising science and reform, that underlay the engineering of the tunnel. The Fu-Ma road was the first class one highway in Fujian. Its opening made an important contribution to Mawei economic development zone

In March, 1986, Xiang Nan (right) meets the vice-chairman of the standing committee of the NPC, the Panchen Lama, Erdeni Choekyi Gyaltsen (centre)

This visit marked an important political exchange between the CPC and the Democratic Socialist Party of the Federal Republic of Germany. Hu Qili and Xiang Nan and their delegation met with the honorary chairman of the party, Willy Brandt, and the German Chancellor Helmut Kohl. They toured the Black Forest and the Saar, visited the advanced KKG nuclear power plant, examined the German vocational education system, called upon the Marxism research centre, and settled on the agenda for the visit to Germany of CPC General Secretary Hu Yaobang.

In the spring of 1986, the party centre named Chen Guangyi to succeed Xiang Nan as secretary of the Fujian Communist Party Committee. Although it had already circulated once officially announced, the news was received with shock by most people in Fujian. Some people linked Xiang Nan's departure to the 'Jinjiang fake drugs' case, concluding that Xiang Nan had been linked to the affair. A number of newspapers overseas published articles indicating their mystification and regret at the news.

By this time, Xiang Nan was already 67. He was one of the longest-serving chief figures among all the provinces, autonomous regions and centrally-administered cities. The arrangements for his departure were normal. Xiang Nan himself showed that he was completely at peace with it. He saw nothing untoward in this arrangement and sincerely hoped that a younger person could take his place, so that Fujian's great enterprise of reform and opening up could continue to advance.

Xiang Nan's successor was formerly the deputy secretary of the Gansu provincial party committee and the province's executive vice-governor. In the early summer of 1986, Xiang Nan turned over the reins to Chen Guangyi and accompanied him on a fact-finding visit to Quanzhou, Xiamen and other places in Fujian. He joined Chen observing the comrades taking part in the third plenum of the sixth Xiamen municipal Communist Party committee, and offered remarks entitled 'I hope that Xiamen will stand at the forefront of the Four Modernisations in Fujian'. At a meeting of responsible cadres from organs that reported directly to the provincial government, Xiang Nan warmly introduced the new party secretary, and made a heartwarming farewell speech. What left him most uneasy was the possibility that some reformers might sustain setbacks at a time when the entire reform and opening up process was still in its earliest stages.

Xiang Nan with Rong Yiren, vice-chairman of the NPC standing committee, in Fuzhou during Rong's inspection visit to Fujian, 1986

With Deep Feeling, Bidding Farewell to Fujian at 67

Xiang Nan hands over the work tasks to the new party secretary, Chen Guangyi, March 1986

Xiang Nan, Wang Zhixin and members of their family on holiday in Beidaihe. From left to right: Liu Ping (their daughter-in-law), Nannan, Beibei, Xiang Nan, Xiaoxiao, Lianlian, Hongwa and Wang Zhixin, 1988

Xiang Nan in Beidaihe, 1987

With Deep Feeling, Bidding Farewell to Fujian at 67

Xiang Nan and Wang Zhixin ascend the Great Wall, 1987

Xiang Nan with his granddaughter Beibei in Beijing, on the eve of her departure to the US for study, April 1994

Xiang Nan and Wang Zhixin at the Leaning Tower of Pisa, 1989

With Deep Feeling, Bidding Farewell to Fujian at 67

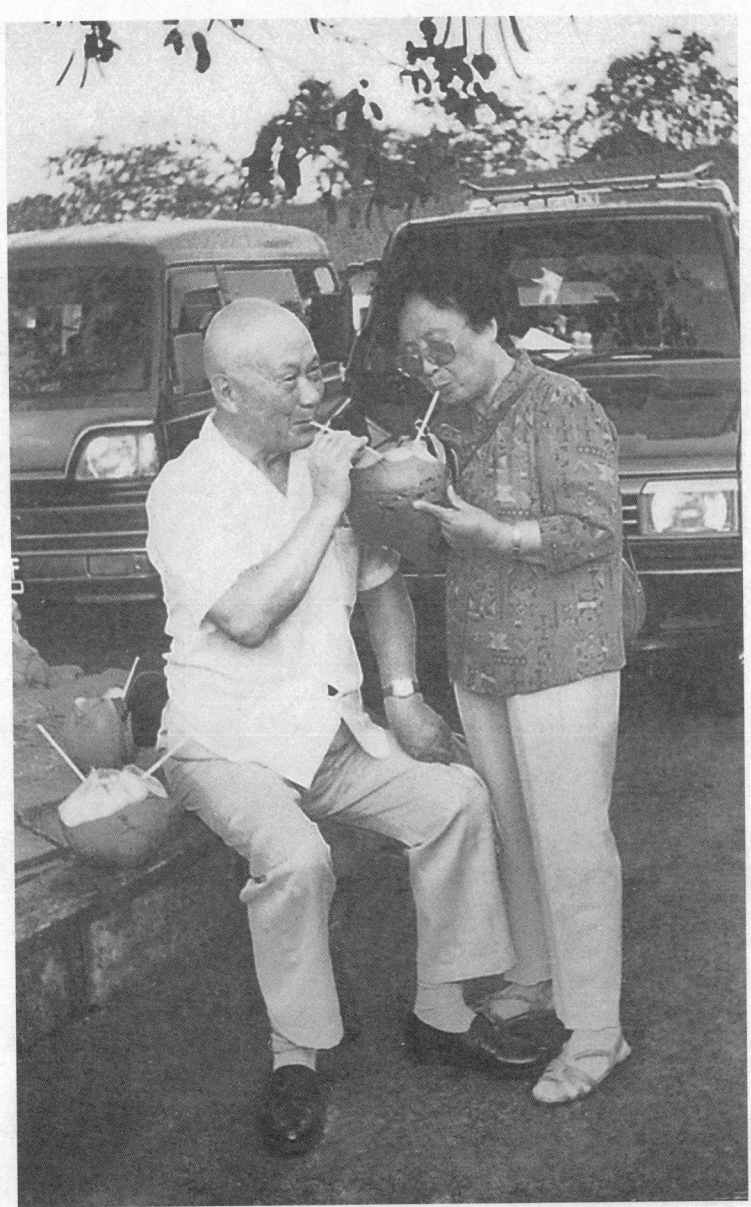

Xiang Nan and Wang Zhixin in Indonesia, 1993

Xiang Nan and Wang Zhixin in a bamboo grove in their native countryside, 1994

Chapter 41

Founding and Leading the China Foundation for the Alleviation of Poverty

In early 1989, Li Xiannian, who had just stepped down from the post of state chairman and had assumed the position of chairman of the CPPCC, called Xiang Nan in for a meeting and asked him to become president of the China Foundation for the Alleviation of Poverty (CFAP).

The CFAP was established on 13 March 1989. Li Xiannian, former state president and former chairman of the CPPPC, became honorary president, and Xiang Nan was elected as the first president. The photo shows Song Renqiong (far left), Li Xiannian (second from left) and Xiang Nan (third from left) at the meeting to establish the foundation (photo by Xu Xiaorong)

Li Xiannian (third from right) and Xiang Nan (second from right) at the meeting to establish the CFAP

The CFAP was established in March 1989. Li Xiannian, chairman of the CPPPC, was named honorary chairman of the foundation, and Xiang Nan was named president. Wei Yuming, Ke Hua, He Zai, Li Ben and Jin Xiying became vice-presidents.

China had only been travelling on the path to reform for less than a decade, and solving the basic problems of food and clothing for the vast majority of the populace had only just been achieved. The problem that arose from this was how to free even more people from poverty. According to prevailing international standards, 1.2bn Chinese people still lived below the poverty line. The Chinese government set a goal of building a modestly prosperous society by the end of the 20th century; if the poverty problem were not solved for that vast number of people, it was idle to speak of a modestly prosperous society. In establishing the CFAP, the goal was to mobilise all possible forces within society in order to help the government

Xiang Nan works on poverty alleviation at the grassroots level

to achieve a basic resolution of the food and clothing challenge for the impoverished population by the end of the 20th century.

As honorary chairman of the CFAP, Li Xiannian was deeply concerned with its work. Even just a few days before his death, he still was receiving reports on the foundation's work. He said gravely to Xiang Nan: "During the war, in the old base districts, the people gave everything they had to us, even letting us eat their precious piglets. Now the revolution has succeeded, we must never, ever forget them."

After the CFAP was created, the first figure to set up a meeting with Xiang Nan was Marshal Nie Rongzhen. After a lifetime of military service, the marshal was by this time bedridden. He knew that his days were numbered, and one of the matters that left him unsettled was that the people in the Taihang mountain liberated area within Jinchaji military district during the anti-Japanese war were still living in deep poverty. He implored Xiang Nan to make sure to help the people in this area escape from poverty into prosperity. Xiang Nan gripped Nie Rongzhen's hands with feeling, and helped the old marshal to set his mind at ease.

Xiang Nan (third from left) with CFAP Vice-President He Zai (far right) and Vice-President Li Jing (second from right), on a visit to the old liberated area in northern Shaanxi

Xiang Nan (third from right) with CFAP Vice-Presidents He Zai (second from left) and Li Jing (second from right) in the old liberated area of Fuping, Hebei province

After his meeting with Marshal Nie, Xiang Nan came to realise what a heavy burden had been placed on his shoulders. Starting a foundation like this from nothing, in order to assist a billion people to escape from destitution, Xiang Nan realised, was a noble but formidable task.

What made the CFAP different from the major global foundations was that 'the CFAP is a foundation without any funds'. The foundation's aim was the alleviation of poverty, and this was the vision that Xiang Nan described in the early stages of its establishment. The ministry of agriculture contributed Rmb100,000 as startup money, and the foundation hung out its

Xiang Nan leading a CFAP group on an inspection in the countryside

Xiang Nan visits the masses in the old Taihang mountain liberated area

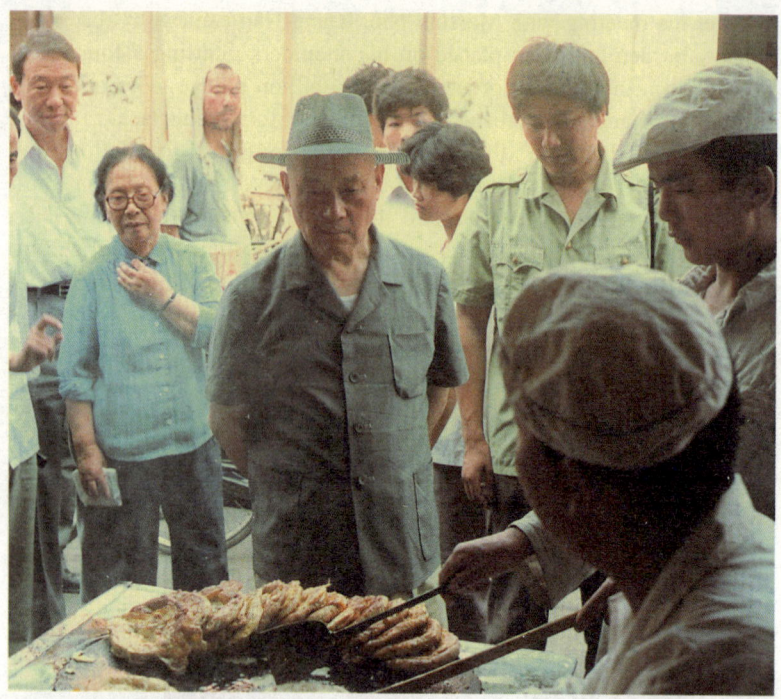

Visiting the old Taihang mountain liberated area, Xiang Nan and Wang Zhixin pay a call on a rural collective trading market

shingle. The only place it conducted business was in a single rented office room in Guanyuan, in Beijing. The first meeting of the foundation's council convened in Xiang Nan's own home. At one point, the CFAP only had Rmb40,000 to its name to carry out its work.

Raising money is a top priority for any foundation. To this end, Xiang Nan created something called the 'Three-character classic of poverty alleviation', following the literary formula of three-character phrases used in one of China's most familiar teaching books for young children. Xiang Nan's aphorisms included: "Only serve, don't seek profit", "Only assist, don't substitute", "Generate more blood, transfuse less", "Open up more, provide relief less", "To escape poverty, rely on oneself, to reach prosperity, rely on science and technology".

This difficult working environment, furthermore, did not drive away the dedicated CFAP work staff, who willingly made their contributions to the work of the foundation. Over 10 years, staff turnover remained low. Many people gave of themselves to the CFAP without publicity or fanfare.

The first tranche of funds that Xiang Nan and old comrades in the CFAP managed to raise went to the Yan'an liberated area. Then, bearing in mind Marshal Nie Rongzhen's appeal, he conducted an on-the-ground look at Fuping county in Hebei province, where he assisted the county party committee and the county government in designing a plan for long-term progress from poverty to prosperity.

Xiang Nan distributes book bags and writing implements to children attending a school for the impoverished

Xiang Nan prepares an inscription for the Liancheng Pengkou middle school in Fujian, 1994

Xiang Nan relied on his personal powers of attraction and his incorruptible work style, as well as his clout and sympathetic appeal among overseas Chinese from Hong Kong, Macau, Taiwan and southeast Asia, and was soon able to bring in a fair number of charitable donations, providing a boost to the CFAP's work. In its early period, the foundation broadened its friendly outreach, strengthened its contacts, and worked strenuously to build understanding and support of its poverty-alleviation efforts among all manner of people inside China and abroad. This became a vital method of continually uncovering new channels of funding for the foundation.

In the eight years of Xiang Nan's leadership of the CFAP, the foundation established regular relationships with more than 60 non-profit organisations and their China-based entities, through a combination of conferences, delegation visits abroad, visits to China by invited delegations, and various other forms of domestic and international exchanges.

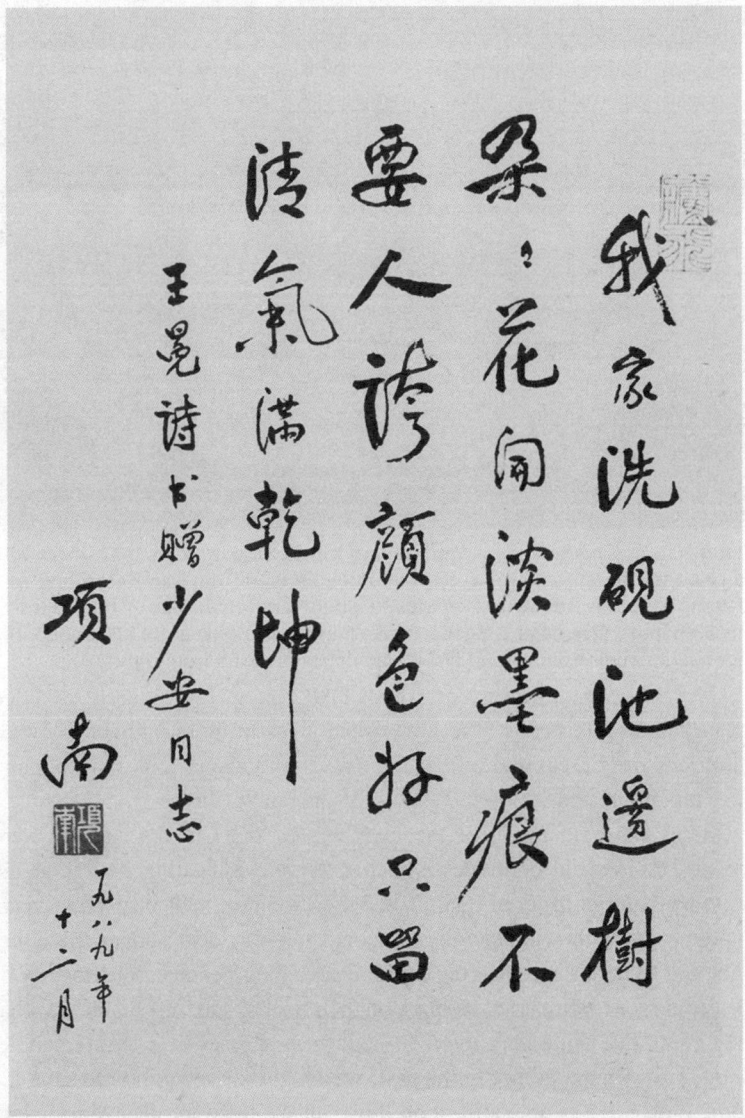

Wang Mian's poem *Plum Blossom* handwritten by Xian Nan: 'In the pond the brushes and ink stone I clean / The trees above it all pale — dark blossoms bear. / For praise of fair colours they appear not to care / But leave to the vast universe their scents serene'

Xiang Nan and his wife on a fund-raising trip to Singapore in 1993, meet with Tan Keong Choon (far left), a member of the family of Tan Kah Kee, along with Li Seng Gee, the renowned charitable donor and chairman of the board of the Singapore Overseas Chinese Bank (third from right) and Li Shangda, the Indonesian businessman and charitable donor (second from right)

Over the years of his service to the CFAP, Xiang Nan regularly travelled on fact-finding missions to impoverished areas in the old liberated areas, ethnic minority areas and border regions. His footsteps took him to many poor mountain areas in northwest, north and south China.

Xiang Nan and many of the members of the CFAP's council were recently retired old comrades who had served as leading figures at the provincial and ministerial rank. When they went on their inspection visits to poor regions, they did their best not to disturb the local leaders, travelling light and trying as hard as they could to save their pennies. The poverty of the ordinary people carved its mark on their hearts, and they pondered what they could do, while they lived, to help these masses of destitute people. They said with emotion: "In the past, we fought the revolution to save the poor. With these people still poor, how can we hope to meet Marx when we die?"

Once, Xiang Nan and CFAP Vice-President He Zai were on the way from Shaanxi to Henan on a fact-finding trip. After leaving southern

In 1995, Xiang Nan, Lei Jieqiong, vice-chairman of the standing committee of the NPC (third from left), and Wang Guangmei (second from left) meet with Li Luda and his wife (fourth and fifth from left)

Shaanxi, they took a long-distance bus into the Qinba mountain district. Their fellow passengers had no idea that these two men over 70, dressed in simple clothes, were senior leaders from Beijing. Along the way, they chatted and joked. It was only after the bus had been in Henan for more than half a day, when it was met by a police car, and local officials invited these two unexpected guests to alight, that the other passengers realised the two old fellows had 'connections'.

In 1994, the state launched the '8-7 poverty alleviation programme'. To coordinate its work with this plan, the CFAP under Xiang Nan's leadership convened three 'poverty alleviation action conferences', in 1994, 1995 and 1996, issuing a 'call for everyone to join in poverty-alleviation work'. At this time, when Xiang Nan, in the twilight of his life, threw himself fully into the anti-poverty work that he loved so deeply and resolved to "bring poverty alleviation to every household", he was once more enshrouded in ill-founded controversy. A number of people maliciously set out to damage the foundation. All this left Xiang Nan feeling deeply fatigued.

Starting in 1995, Xiang Nan was repeatedly hospitalised with heart ailments, and his physicians and family members urged him to rest. But this man, who never rested, continued to pursue his work every day, just as he had always done with the CFAP. His children said of him: "Even when conversation turned to those times when he had been treated most unfairly, he never felt sorry for himself. He only fretted about his country and his people. He said with enormous sadness: 'We wasted too much time! If, 30 or 20 or even 10 years earlier, we had given the nation and the people a decent environment, we could have accomplished so many things, and the gap between China and the rest of the world would not seem so great'."

Had it not been for a sudden heart attack, Xiang Nan had been planning to go on fact-finding missions to a number of places. He had often expressed the wish that, in his lifetime, he would be able to visit typically impoverished areas in all parts of China – east and west, north and south – so as to help in the planning and the policy-making for the great anti-poverty effort, and so as to help more people and businesses join the ranks of those fighting poverty in China, making every possible effort to allow even more people from poor areas to throw off the bonds of poverty…

Chapter 42

A Monument to the Alleviation of Poverty Stands in People's Hearts

After the CFAP had been operating for seven or eight years, it had provided money and material support to impoverished districts and impoverished families amounting to Rmb600m, bringing benefits to more than 1.6m poor rural dwellers. The foundation had also set in motion a number of anti-poverty projects, strengthening the ability of poor peasant households to fend for themselves, developing their own abilities and making it possible for them, on receiving one-time financial support, to reap long-lasting benefits.

Xiang Nan, Li Shangda and Li Luda at the ribbon-cutting for the Cishan school, built with the Li brothers' donations

Xiang Nan paid close attention to helping the poor people of western Fujian become prosperous. Here, he inspects a rural enterprise in western Fujian

One of the CFAP's major projects in its early years was the building of linkages between cadres in two locations far from one another: Jiangsu and Shaanxi provinces. The foundation could not wait until it had sufficient funds before beginning its work, and so, building on the linkages among veteran comrades, it began constructing a network of 140 counterparts in Jiangsu and Shaanxi. This project took a year, and involved as many as 200 schemes in southern Shaanxi. Ultimately, the project raised Rmb10m and involved as many as 500 people. With information and help provided by their cadre counterparts in Jiangsu, southern Shaanxi was able to market nearly 100 of its products, worth more than Rmb70m, to coastal areas of China and to international markets.

This kind of cadre-to-cadre exchange won support and further expansion from the organisation department at the party centre and from the state council's leading small group on poverty alleviation, and quickly grew to encompass 29 provinces and autonomous regions, as well as more than 10,000 cadres. State leaders honoured the program with the phrase: 'A pioneering undertaking in poverty alleviation.'

A Monument to the Alleviation of Poverty Stands in People's Hearts

Xiang Nan inspects a soil conservation project along the Changting river in Fujian

Xiang Nan visits impoverished residents in the west Fujian former base area, 1994

Xiang Nan with Liu Weican (far left), former chair of the Huamei Cigarette plant and a warm supporter of poverty alleviation work, in western Fujian, 1994

Xiang Nan attends the opening ceremony of the Shaanxi-Jiangsu cadre exchange training session

Xiang Nan mobilised all kinds of forces within society to join in the anti-poverty effort. From 1994 on, the foundation supported more than 40 training courses for county- township- and village-level cadres, covering more than 4,000 people, and conducted by model workers such as Wu Renbao, Zhang Zhenliang, Shi Laihe and Chang Zonglin in places such as Huaxi village in Jiangsu, Doudian village in Beijing, Liuzhuang in Henan, Zhangjiagang in Jiangsu, Wuxi and Weifang in Shandong, Mouping, Longkou and Xiamen in Fujian.

In wide-ranging cooperation with the media, the influence of the anti-poverty effort brought broader results. Beginning in 1994, the CFAP and the media conducted annual concentrated publicity campaigns. The foundation, Xinhua news agency and the publishers of a leading bi-weekly magazine jointly organised an annual contest to select the 10 best anti-poverty leaders from throughout the nation. That contest was held seven times, and 70 'anti-poverty champions' were selected.

Inviting science and technology specialists to go into impoverished regions to help propagate the anti-poverty programme that went by the motto 'short, equal and fast', was an especially important element in CFAP's science and technology effort in those regions. The technologies that the foundation used in its efforts to expand the process of moving villages from destitution to prosperity included *juncao* planting technology, the Long method of raising pigs, Nande tropical cattle, short-tailed cold-weather sheep and other breeding techniques. Among these, the *juncao* planting technology transformed the traditional

Xiang Nan takes part in a ceremony marking the departure of the first 'little reporters poverty work delegation'

Lei Jieqiong, member of the standing committee of the NPC (second from left) attends the CFAP anti-poverty action conference led by Xiang Nan, 1995

Xiang Nan chairs the opening session of the China anti-poverty action conference, 1994

methods of using wood material such as sawdust as the substrate for the cultivation of fungi, and made possible the use of all sorts of wild grasses, sea grasses and straw from economic crops to cultivate both edible and medicinal fungi. The discoverer of this technology was the Fujian Agricultural University professor Lin Zhanxi, who donated the technology, without any financial reward, to the CFAP. The foundation placed great emphasis on the popularisation of this technology, and established training bases at Fujian Agriculture University, in Beijing's Daxing county and in Chengdu, Sichuan province. In all, the CFAP carried out 70 core training courses on *juncao* techniques, covering 4,800 trainees in 29 provinces and regions, and 328 counties, and bringing benefits to 35,500 households engaged in the cultivation of edible and medicinal fungi.

The CFAP also engaged with Japan's Sasakawa peace foundation to conduct a series of five annual training sessions in Shibing county, Guizhou province, emphasising new planting and cultivation techniques. Thanks to a contribution of Rmb10m from the Chinese American Li

Xiang Nan leads a CFAP delegation to the US to learn about the operations of American nonprofit charitable organisations, 1995

Xiang Nan converses with US nonprofit charitable organisation figures, 1995

Lingyu, the foundation was able to bring primary school students from impoverished districts to study in special technical middle schools; they returned to their homes as core figures in the effort to advance from poverty to prosperity.

From the establishment of the CFAP to Xiang Nan's departure in 1997, China's nongovernmental anti-poverty enterprise went from having nothing to being well established. The *Chronicle of Major Events at the CFAP* records 100 major events over an eight-year period. These events are the great footprints left behind from the foundation's arduous struggle, under Xiang Nan's leadership, to move ahead.

After Xiang Nan's death, the first commemorative monument erected in his memory was not in his native countryside, but rather at the Prosperous People's school in Fuping county, deep in the Taihang mountains of Hebei province. That small monument is evidence of the first anti-poverty efforts of Xiang Nan and the foundation. On the reverse side of the stone monument is the figure of Xiang Nan, as soaring as the Taihang mountains themselves.

A Monument to the Alleviation of Poverty Stands in People's Hearts

Xiang Nan at the memorial to Dr Martin Luther King, leader of the movement for African American civil rights, April 1995

Xiang Nan at the United Nations in New York, 1995

Xiang Nan and his wife congratulate the universally beloved Zhang Yun on her 90th birthday in 1995

A Monument to the Alleviation of Poverty Stands in People's Hearts

Xiang Nan and Wan Weisheng, the master designer of postage stamps

Xiang Nan always got up at the break of day, and studied endlessly. To the very last days of his life, he remained deeply concerned with the struggles of ordinary people, and with the future and destiny of the nation

Xiang Nan, in hospital, received Xia Meng (left), the director of the documentary film *The Loyal Souls of Mother Earth*, 1996. On the right is Yang Xiao

A few days before his death, Xiang Nan receives at his residence the young Fujian author Zhong Zhaoyun, November 1997

A Monument to the Alleviation of Poverty Stands in People's Hearts

While participating in the 15th CPC congress, Xiang Nan drafted the main points of a statement by a leading small group, 1997 (photo by Yang Zhishuan)

Xiang Nan in Beijing, 1997. Xiang spent the final years and months of his life contributing to China's poverty-alleviation efforts. To the last, he continued to spend all his mental energy on his poverty-alleviation work

Wang Zhixin in Wenfang village, Pengkou township, Liancheng county, Xiang Nan's native place, December 2001 (photo by Yang Zhishuan)

The successive party secretaries of Fujian pay a visit to Wang Zhixin in 2002. From left to right: Chen Mingyi, Chen Guangyi, Wang Zhixin, Jia Qinglin and Song Defu (photo by Yang Zhishuan)

A Monument to the Alleviation of Poverty Stands in People's Hearts

Xiang Nan was the first provincial party secretary to build an expressway. As early as 1981, he raised his idea of building a high-speed highway from Fuzhou to Xiamen, and set about developing the necessary plans and implementing steps. That dream only began to see fulfilment after Xiang Nan's death. Fujian has now basically completed a web of three north-south and three east-west expressways, and is among the provinces with the most concentrated network of high-speed roads

The Shikong mountain bridge on the Zhangzhou-Longyan expressway

Xiang Nan: Champion of Reform in Fujian

In Xiang Nan's native place of Liancheng county, there is a mystical hill named Guanzhi. On Xiang Nan's 90th birthday, thanks to a donation from the overseas Chinese leader Li Luda, his fellow countrymen built this 'Pure Spirit pavilion' where weary travellers might rest. They also erected a stone monument, inscribed with a poem by the Buddhist master Zhao Puchu, written in the master's own hand, and entitled *Elegy to Comrade Xiang Nan*. On the pavilion, the three words 'Pure Spirit pavilion' were written by the master scholar of Chinese studies Rao Zongyi, while the inscription, 'In heaven and earth, the spirit is pure / In rivers and mountains, the sun does not set' was inscribed by Pan Zhulan, a master of the ancient Golden Stone form of calligraphy. In one corner of the Pure Spirit pavilion an inscription in Xiang Nan's own writing reads: 'No one need boast of the excellent colours here / All that matters is that a pure spirit fills heaven and earth'. These were two lines from a poem found on Plum Blossoms by the Yuan dynasty painter Wang Mian. Xiang Nan often took these two lines when presenting gifts of his calligraphy. This square four-cornered cooling pavilion, under the name 'pure spirit', is without doubt the best memorial to Xiang Nan

A Monument to the Alleviation of Poverty Stands in People's Hearts

The original calligraphy of Master Zhao Puchu's *Elegy to Comrade Xiang Nan*

《项南同志哀辞》
赵朴初
一九九七年十一月

四十三年前，与君初相识。	意态惊英发，	言辞喜真挚，	及君主闽政，我偶访榕州。
相见辄欢喜，劝我南山游。	渊识谈所见，	为我解烦忧。	今行众意倒，
岁月去如飞，我已鬓重斑。	病身托医院，	不意君亦至，	朝夕相过从，谈笑如畴昔。
如我念家乡，太湖贫困邑，	为等千万元，	同济饥家急。	忠爱与友情，众我感愧泣。
君年少于我，体魄尚魁梧，	方期百岁寿，	同倾甘露壶。	孰知偏视忤，君竟撒手别，
岂惟丧友悲，闽民同泣血。	君生有自来，	世代传功烈，	铁骨甘百折，
山路任漫漫，登攀无断绝。	君今逢盛世，	且为尽心力，	一瞑应无憾，千载留勋绩。

注释赵朴老《项南同志哀辞》
汪志馨

Zhao Puchu's elegy to the late Xiang Nan, and Wang Zhixin's accompanying annotation

Epilogue

On 10 November 1997, the superb CPC member, loyal and sincere fighter for communism through long experience, member of the 13th central advisory commission, founding president and principal advisor of the CFAP, former secretary of the Fujian provincial Communist Party committee, former first political commissar of Fujian provincial military district, Xiang Nan, was stricken by a sudden heart attack. Attempts to revive him were unsuccessful, and he regrettably passed away in Beijing at the age of 79.

At 5am, Xiang Nan had arisen as usual and, after brief exercises, had begun to read books and other writings. In the morning he went to the hospital for a checkup, and in the afternoon a leading figure from the Fujian party committee paid a visit. They talked until 5pm. Then Xiang Nan and his wife departed for the Wangfu hotel to greet a group of foreign friends who were connected to the CFAP. After dining there, they went to the China World hotel to meet a leading overseas Chinese figure. They chatted until 10pm, when Xiang Nan felt ill and asked his wife beside him for some medicine. Just as he stood up, before the water glass reached his hand, he suddenly sat down, and departed this world.

Xiang Nan's death aroused a strong response at home and abroad. Especially in the hearts of the broad masses of Fujian, Xiang Nan had stood as a mighty tree. People would not forget his contributions to reform and opening up. He was a representative figure of his era. He devoted himself to thought but was a courageous man of action. Many of his visions and viewpoints led the way for our era. He played an important role in advancing historical progress in a transitional era.

Epilogue

In 2008, *Southern Metropolitan Daily* published a collection of essays on 30 stormy figures from three decades of reform and opening up. Xiang Nan was one of the thirty. *Southern Weekend*, under the title 'Eight Sages of Reform', discussed eight reformist figures who had influenced the historical advancement of reform and opening up; Xiang Nan was one of those eight. From this we can say that calling him a pioneer of reform and opening up is in no way an exaggeration.

Chronology of Major Events in the Life of Xiang Nan

1918

18 November: Born in Wendi village, Pengkou township, Liancheng county, Fujian province. Given the name Xiang Dechong. Aged five, entered private traditional school. First teacher was Xiang Jishen

1929

Sixth uncle Xiang Tingji became propaganda worker in Red Guards. Aged 11, became head of the young pioneers brigade

1930

April: Xiang Tingji, aged 24, killed in the line of duty

Autumn: Wang Cunyu, mother of Xiang Nan, guided by transport worker Xie Zhizhong, takes Xiang Nan and younger sister from Liancheng county to Shanghai

1931

Entered Yaohuamen school in Nanjing as fifth grade student. Xiang Nan's primary school graduation exam essay ranked first among all primary school graduation essays in Nanjing's Jiangning county

1932

After graduation from Yaohuamen primary school, entered Shanghai Qiangshu Garden arts half-work/half-study school in Shanghai. After graduation, performed miscellaneous tasks at *National News*, published three times a month under auspices of the China vocational education society

1934

March: Xiang Nan's father Xiang Yunian sent to the security headquarters of the fourth district, northern Jiangxi, as intelligence staff

September: Xiang Yunan braved death to transmit secret intelligence to the Jiangxi soviet

1935

Wang Cunyu arrested in Shanghai while guarding the CPC party centre's secret radio transmitter. Younger sister incarcerated with her mother. Six months later, escaped from jail with help of party underground. Mother took younger sister back to home territory. Soon after, younger sister died from tuberculosis of the bone, as result of imprisonment

1937

Finished sojourn at Shanghai Qiangshu Garden arts school. Introduced to Changle county, Fujian province plant nursery for horticultural job

After July 7 Incident, organised 'Tomorrow Singing Troupe', becomes deputy troupe leader, carries out propaganda for resistance to Japan and for national salvation

1938

Wang Zhu, head of Fujian provincial party committee propaganda department, invited Xiang Nan to chat at Fujian youth society, secretly recruited Xiang Nan to party membership

'Tomorrow Singing Troupe' disbanded. Xiang Nan did horticultural work in Shunchang county, northern Fujian; edited county bulletin, created 'Shunchang Resist the Enemy Theatre Troupe' and became troupe leader. Suspected by local authorities of communist membership. Secretly tipped off by countryman Luo Xinru, Xiang Nan escaped

1939

Late spring or early summer: Changed name to Xiang Xin. At introduction of friend Huang Kaixiu, started 'Minqing county government wartime mobile work team for popular education' in Minqing county. Served as team leader; Huang Kaixiu as team guide

August: Shifted to Nanping and then to Guilin in Guangxi to evade capture. With assistance from Eighth Route Army office in Guilin, transferred to Yan'an

1940

Moved to Beijing to teach at Chengda normal school. Fired for teaching and singing progressive songs. Aided by fellow countrymen Zhang Xuecheng and Yuan Nantian, returned to Guilin as provisional director of Lingui county plant nursery

1941

Through Eighth Route Army arrangements, transferred to Hong Kong. Through Liao Chengzhi's arrangements there, transfered to New Fourth Army headquarters in Yancheng, north Jiangsu province

Late summer/early autumn: Assigned by party centre's central China bureau as political commissar in Yanfu district. Changed name to Xiang Nan. Unable to prove party membership, took party membership for second time in northern Jiangsu, without normal mandatory waiting period

1942

Secretary to Fudong county (now called Binhai county, Jiangsu province) government. Wang Zhixin assigned to Fudong ninth district from Number 5 School of War of Resistance University to serve as propaganda worker and district head. Xiang Nan soon transferred to ninth district as party secretary

1943

Led ninth district inhabitants and armed forces in counter-assault on large-scale Japanese cleanup campaign launched against anti-Japanese resistance base in ninth district

1944

Married Wang Zhixin. First son Xiang Xiaohong born at end of year. Participated in rectification movement study. Subjected to criticism for being unable to explain father Xiang Yunian's social connections and political complexion

1945

Victory in War of Resistance. Transferred to fifth special administrative headquarters, northern Jiangsu, as reconstruction department head

1946

October: In mortal peril, transferred to northern Jiangsu support headquarters as head of supply unit. Distinguished himself in behind-the-lines support work during the Lianshui battle, earned praise from leaders of central China military zone

1947

Became head of the finance and economic office of the 11th special administrative headquarters, northern Jiangsu. Other posts included party secretary of cadre school, Jianghuai district; deputy chief of propaganda unit, CPC Chu county committee; deputy secretary of CPC Dongnan county committee and concurrently political commissar with Dongnan armed unit

1948

March: Participated in battle to recover Huainan

June: Appointed party secretary, Jianghuai district cadre school, and director of education, Jianghuai public school

July: Transferred to become deputy secretary of CPC Dongnan county committee and political commissar of Dongnan armed unit

End of year: Headed propaganda section of Jianghuai prefectural party committee

1949

By recommendation of Tan Zhenlin, deputy political commissar, east China military district, joined Huang Xinbai and Liu Xing as north Anhui representatives at China New Democracy Youth League first national congress, convened 11 April. Met Mao Zedong, Zhu De, Ren Bishi and other central leaders. Soon, became party secretary for northern Anhui working committee of youth league

1950

May: Establishment of north Anhui Democratic Youth League. Elected chairman

1951

Seeking to help old wartime comrade Liang Mingde locate his lost son, north Anhui district CPC secretary Zeng Xisheng established contact between Xiang Nan and his father Liang Mingde (Xiang Yunian) after 20 years

1952

Early: Establishment of Anhui committee of the Democratic Youth League. Xiang Nan became secretary to league provincial committee and party secretary of Anhui University

1953

Became second secretary of youth league east China committee. Moved with family to Shanghai. Found mother Wang Cunyu and brought her into the Shanghai family

1954

March: Took part in USSR communist youth league 12th congress. Published *Diary of Visit to the USSR* in *Shanghai Youth Daily*. Later republished by Shanghai People's Publishing House

September: Elected member of NPC representing Anhui. Participated in first NPC

1955

February: Travelled with Wang Zhixin to see father in Shenyang. Brought Shanghai family to Beijing

Became chief of central propaganda department of China New Democracy Youth League. Wang Zhixin became deputy head of the league's central teenage youth department

1956

May: Fact-finding mission to the three northeastern provinces with Hu Yaobang, youth league first party secretary

September: Elected delegate to eighth party congress, attended CPC eighth party congress. On eve of youth league third congress, drafted *Ten Opinions* document for league leadership

1957

May: Third congress of CYL convened. Elected member of CYL central secretariat

June: Acting as vice chairman of All-China Youth Federation, led China youth delegation on visit to Japan

July: World youth festival opened in Moscow. CYL delegation led by Hu Yaobang, with Xiang Nan, Wu Xueqian and Ma Yuehan as deputy leaders, attended festival. More than 1,000 in the delegation

September: En route home from USSR, passed through Xinjiang and Gansu. Fact-finding visits examined youth league work in Yili, Urumqi, etc

Chronology of Major Events in the Life of Xiang Nan

1958

Ten Opinions singled out and criticised by Kang Sheng for deviation from high principles

June-August: Third plenum of third CYL central committee convened. Xiang Nan declared a 'rightist element' and severely criticised. Full plenary meeting removed Xiang Nan from league standing committee and position in secretariat as well as from position as head of publicity department. On eve of national day, sent away to Beijing Dongjiao state farm for labour. Party membership placed on probation for two years

1959

After Lushan plenum, demoted two administrative ranks

1960

Dongjiao state farm renamed Sino-Albanian friendship people's commune. Xiang Nan made deputy commune leader. Actively supported disbandment of communal dining halls

1961

At Hu Yaobang's recommendation and with permission from party central organisation department, became deputy chief of administrative office of eighth ministry of machine building

1962

Served as head of agricultural machinery bureau, eighth ministry of machine building

September-December: issued articles entitled 'Agricultural equipment research work should stand at the forefront of agricultural mechanisation', 'What we have seen and heard regarding rural wheelbarrows', 'Accelerate technical transformation of agricultural equipment making enterprises' and 'Some questions concerning agricultural mechanisation

1964

1963-1964: Led work teams on fact-finding trips to nine provinces, municipalities and autonomous regions to inspect conditions in agriculture and agricultural mechanisation

1965

Issued *Report on Investigation of Questions of Agricultural Mechanisation*

1966

February: Participated in planning and leading of national agricultural mechanisation management planning conference. Presented report *Use Mao Zedong Thought as Overall Guide, Reach Beyond Other Countries' Experiences, March Along Our Own Path*

1967

Investigated and accused by rebel faction in eighth ministry, seized and subjected to 'struggle'

1968

Entered 'study group', subjected to 'supervision by the masses', underwent labour reform

1969

August: Sent down to May 7 cadre school of the eighth ministry in Yilan county, Heilongjiang province

November: Relocated to May 7 cadre school in Xinyang, Henan province

1970

Freed and made head of agricultural machinery small group in first ministry of machine building and head of agricultural machinery bureau in the first ministry

1971-1975

Successively served as member of party core small group in first ministry, head of agricultural machinery bureau

1975: Joined in preparatory work on national conference on 'In agriculture, learn from Dazhai'

1976

August: Led 15-person fact-finding group to the US to examine agriculture and agricultural mechanisation

October: On returning to China, completed writing of *Investigative Report on US Agricultural Mechanisation*

December: Participated in planning for second national 'In agriculture, learn from Dazhai' conference

1977

August: Reported results of US fact-finding mission to the party centre and state council leaders, receiving high attention

September: Became vice-minister of first ministry of machine building and member of party core small group

1978

April: Led team to Europe for investigation of agriculture and agricultural mechanisation in Italy, France, the UK and Denmark. After return, supervised the writing of articles and reports including *Discussion of Agricultural Modernisation After Return from Four-Country Fact-Finding Mission*

October: Father Xiang Yunian died in Longyan, Fujian, after illness and hospitalisation, at 82. Xiang Nan participated in commemorative ceremonies at CPC Liaoning party committee and provincial revolutionary committee

1979

Executive vice minister of ministry of agricultural mechanisation and secretary of the party committee. Elected delegate to fifth NPC

May: Ministry of agricultural mechanisation and central youth league announced approval by the party centre of *Report Regarding Comrade Xiang Nan's Rehabilitation*

June: Led Chinese agricultural mechanisation delegation to the Philippines, Australia, Hong Kong and Singapore

December: Led working group research trip to Jiangsu and Shanghai

1980

3 September: Participated in UNIDO Beijing cooperative conference on exchange of lessons learned in the agricultural equipment industry. Presented address on behalf of PRC government

December: Appointed member of Fujian provincial party committee and member of its standing committee

1981

14 January: Took office in Fuzhou

20 January: Conveyed to Fujian provincial party congress the party centre's leadership instructions on Fujian party work. Address entitled 'Discussing emancipation of thought'. Central party leadership appraised Xiang Nan address highly, authorised its distribution to all province-rank officials and army-rank officers

Beginning February: Conducted research visits throughout the province. Worked hard to carry out household contracting and production responsibility systems. Visited Xiamen SEZ, asserted 2.5 square kilometre area insufficient, made case to visit Vice-Premier Gu Mu for expansion of Xiamen SEZ to encompass entire Xiamen island

April: Third plenum of fifth Fujian provincial party congress convened. Xiang Nan made special speech 'Emancipation of thinking and special policies', argued for three main Fujian tasks in 1980s: development of economy, overseas Chinese work and work regarding Taiwan. Raised the idea of Fujian's eight major bases

27 May-14 June: Participated in work conference on SEZs in Guangdong and Fujian, convened by state council in Beijing, and presented important speech

July: Fujian provincial party committee and government decided to set aside 200 square kilometres of unoccupied coastal land to be retained by commune members for shellfish and algae cultivation

August: Pressed the provincial government to issue its decisions designating 13,300 square kilometres of unoccupied mountain land for commune members' retention

September: *Fujian Daily* described 26 rural households from across the province that achieved prosperity through their own hard work. Xiang Nan wrote the article 'In praise of the cream of the crop'

1982

February: Named first secretary of the Fujian CPC committee. Participated in Guangdong-Fujian seminar convened by central party secretariat

March: Attended fourth session of Fujian fifth provincial people's congress. Spoke on 'Confidence and power', called for 10 major engineering projects

April: Pushed forward various documents for the provincial government to promulgate. The provincial government approved the first 48 enterprises to be placed under factory director supervision

July: Delivered address, 'Use one hand for economic tasks and the other hand to deal with big cases' to a conference of Fujian local and city party secretaries

August: In remarks to *People's Daily* reporter, called for attacking economic crimes, greater assistance to commune and brigade enterprises, and distinction between heavy attacks on major economic crimes on one hand and the enlivening of the economy on the other

September: Led Fujian delegation to the 12th party congress. Elected to party central committee

October: Attended national conference on marine aquatics convened by Fujian. Delivered address, 'Bring prosperity to the mountains and the seas'

November: Accompanied CPC General Secretary Hu Yaobang on inspection visit to Xiamen, Fuzhou, Jinjiang, Putian and Ningde

1983

10 March: Pressed provincial party committee and provincial government to issue documents calling for leadership to take steps to implement all forms of operational responsibility systems, with contracts as the core element, and to firmly root out the 'big pot' phenomenon

17 May: Participated in the Chendai commune field meeting of Fujian provincial commune and brigade enterprises. Presented address 'The masses pooling their resources to operate factories is a good thing'. Strongly supported and promoted commune and brigade (township and village) enterprise development, strongly praised the pooling of funds to run factories, calling it 'socialism, not capitalism'

18 September: Speech at Fujian province SEZs conference, 'Create a new situation in our SEZ work as quickly as we can'. Proposed the 'four specials' for SEZs: timely special tasks, special policies, special environments and special methodologies

November: Led a meeting on the administrative work of the provincial party committee secretaries, affirmed further strengthening basic infrastructure construction, announced infrastructure development guidelines for the sixth and seventh five-year plans, affirmed development of the economy of southern Fujian and development of coastal areas native to many overseas Chinese

1984

February: Accompanied Deng Xiaoping to Xiamen. Recommended expansion of Xiamen SEZ to include entire Xiamen island and step-by-step development of free port. Deng wrote inscription, 'May the SEZ be operated even better and even more rapidly'

2 March: Worked hard to establish Xiamen Airlines.

18 March: Party centre decided to expand Xiamen SEZ to cover entire Xiamen island

23 March: Meeting of 55 factory directors and managers in Fuzhou sent message to provincial party committee leaders, calling for 'loosening the shackles' on factories and devolving authority powers to lower administrative levels. Xiang Nan sent the letter to *Fujian Daily* to make it public and wrote his own comment

15-31 May: Led Fujian delegation to second session of sixth NPC

19 May: In address, called for admission of the word 'contract' into vocabulary, destruction of the 'big pot' system in SOEs, close linking of staff and worker pay to quality of enterprise operation and individual contributions

18 May: *Fujian Daily* published Xiang Nan editorial 'Let the word 'contract' enter into our vocabulary'

24 May: *People's Daily* reprinted the 18 May article

11 October: Provincial party standing committee meeting established a leading small group on the handling of problems left over from history relating to the underground party work in Fujian

6 December: Sent congratulatory message to Chendai township in Pujiang on achievement of first 'Rmb100m township' status

1985

18 February: Party centre and state council announced decision creating a coastal economic development zone including 11 counties and cities – Zhangzhou, Longhai, Zhangpu, Dongshan, Quanzhou, Jinjiang, Hui'an, Anxi, Yongchun and Tongan. The result of Xiang Nan's diligent efforts over many years

6 March: At conference on handling problems left over from history relating to the party's underground operations in Fujian, delivered speech demanding basic completion of this work by the end of May

16 June: *People's Daily* ran the famous article 'Riveting and disturbing

fake drug case in Jinjiang, Fujian'. Called provincial party committee administrative office and demanded that relevant units at provincial level, in the Jinjiang district and in Pujiang county firmly investigate and deal with the fake drug case

3 July: Fourth CPC Fujian party committee convened first session. Elected new batch of cadres to form the new party committee. Xiang Nan elected party committee secretary. Hu Ping elected deputy secretary. Standing committee members Jia Qinglin, Zhang Yumin, Gao Hu, Zhang Kehui, Lin Zhize, Cai Ninglin, Yuan Qitong and He Shaochuan

1986

6 February: Accompanied Yang Shangkun, member of the CPC central politburo and vice chairman of standing committee of the central military commission, on a visit to troops, the countryside and factories

24 February: Hu Yaobang and other central leaders met with Xiang Nan to discuss ways of making the Fujian provincial party committee more dynamic

27 February: Party centre appointed Cheng Guangyi as Fujian party secretary, relieved Xiang Nan of his position as secretary in the Fujian provincial party

14-20 March: With Chen Guangyi, visited Xiamen, Zhangzhou, Quanzhou and Putian to deepen understanding of coastal economic conditions. Further explored issues related to the *Classic of Mountains and Seas*

May: Visited western Fujian before departing, to see those dear to him. First return visit to the village of his birth, Wendi, in Pengkou township, Liancheng county

1989

13 March: CFAP established, Li Xiannian, former state president and chairman of the CPPCC, made honorary chairman. Huang Hua and Fei Xiaotong appointed honorary vice-chairs. Xiang Nan elected president. Created 'The three-character classic of poverty alleviation' for the foundation

December: CFAP donated Rmb500,000 to Fujian Anlala citrus project, and Rmb300,000 to Guangdong Zhaoqing district project for improved banana cultivation

1990

April: Accompanied State President Yang Shangkun on visit to Ng Teng Fong, head of Far East Organisation

August: Pursued cooperation between CFAP and British charity Save the Children

1991

February: Led meeting of the CFAP Beijing council standing committee

March: Acted as go-between linking 140 Jiangsu and Shaanxi cadres for counterpart exchanges aimed at assisting poverty alleviation

May: Visited impoverished areas of Hebei with Beijing representative of Israel Academy of Social Sciences, formed cooperative agreement for project on irrigation and training for development of arid and semi-arid regions of north China, including three training classes on water-saving, donations of irrigation equipment, etc

7 July: CFAP sent delegation of SME representatives from impoverished areas to visit Japan, in cooperation with China Association for International Friendly Contacts, using fact-finding activities on poverty relief as organised by Sasekawa Peace and Friendship Foundation

1992

January: Represented CFAP to receive Rmb10m contribution from Zhaotong (Yunnan) Cigarette

May: Attended Beijing conference involving cadres from developed and impoverished regions, introduced experiences gained in Jiangsu-Shaanxi cadre interchange project and advocated an expansion of the programme

1993

April: Led second session of CFAP council in Beijing, summed up work experiences, explored new avenues of CFAP work

4 June: Attended meeting establishing the China Poverty Development Association

October: At invitation of Sasekawa Peace Financial Group and China-Japan Friendship Foundation, organised second delegation of county magistrates from impoverished areas for fact-finding visit to Japan

1994

July: Led delegation of 60 from FCAP and CASS to forum on economic development of central and western China

16 July: Chaired meeting on anti-poverty efforts, received 15 donations, including US$1m gift from Singapore Chinese Li Loke Tai

16 October: Officiated at awards ceremony recognising 10 best poverty-alleviation champions from across China

17 October: Commemoration of first international poverty eradication day through a vast evening cultural performance, 'Love Resides in All of Us', at the Great Hall of the People

November: Travelled to Fuping county, Hebei to officiate at opening ceremonies for vocational education school constructed with Rmb300,000 donated by Li Juneng of Hong Kong Rotary Club

1995

January: Travelled to Laoluqu village, Datai township, 10km from Fuping county seat, to inquire about poverty

April: Led CFAP delegation to the US to learn about operations of nonprofit organisations

May: Officiated at donation of 10 portable B-type ultrasound diagnostic equipment units from Toshiba Sanko Medical Systems Corporation

June: Conducted three training classes at Doudian, in Beijing's Fangshan district, for Shanxi poverty-alleviation. In all, more than 100 people involved in cattle-raising, from Shanxi, Gansu, Ningxia and Hebei received training

July: Attended second national recognition ceremony for nation's 10 top anti-poverty heroes, organised by CFAP, Xinhua news agency and the magazine *Semi-Monthly*

November: Attended opening ceremony for training class on promotion of short-tailed sheep in impoverished regions

1996

4 January: Attended second conference on poverty-alleviation activities, accepted donations of more than Rmb3m and 104 Golden Frog brand farm transport vehicles

February: Attended formal ceremony of CFAP and China Youth Activities

Centre marking embarkation of 'Capital Young Reporters Poverty Alleviation Work Team'

21 May: Served as master of ceremonies at US Exxon Corporation donation of US$500,000

September: CFAP convened third council meeting, passed *Revised Draft of China Poverty Alleviation Foundation Articles*, elected State Vice President Rong Yiren honorary president, CPPCC chairman Yang Rudai as foundation president and Xiang Nan as principal advisor

1997

September: Attended 15th CPC congress, made important speech at meeting of fourth small group

10 November: Passed away in Beijing, aged 79